Hand Drafting
for INTERIOR DESIGN

Hand Drafting
for INTERIOR DESIGN

Diana Bennett Wirtz Kingsley
ASID, IIDA

Jeanne Diehl-Shaffer, Ph.D.
RID, ASID, IIDA, IDEC
SEMINOLE STATE COLLEGE OF FLORIDA
College of Engineering,
Construction, and Design

3RD EDITION

FAIRCHILD BOOKS
NEW YORK · LONDON · OXFORD · NEW DELHI · SYDNEY

FAIRCHILD BOOKS
Bloomsbury Publishing Inc
1385 Broadway, New York, NY 10018, USA
50 Bedford Square, London, WC1B 3DP, UK
29 Earlsfort Terrace, Dublin 2, Ireland

BLOOMSBURY, FAIRCHILD BOOKS and the Fairchild Books logo are trademarks of
Bloomsbury Publishing Plc

First edition published 2010
Second edition published 2014

This edition first published in the United States of America 2020
Reprinted 2020, 2021, 2022

Library of Congress Cataloging-in-Publication Data
Names: Kingsley, Diana, author. | Diehl-Shaffer, Jeanne, 1960- author.
Title: Hand drafting for interior design / Diana Bennett Wirtz Kingsley, ASID, IIDA;
    Jeanne Diehl-Shaffer Ph.D., RID, ASID, IIDA, IDEC, Seminole State College of
    Florida, College of Engineering, Construction, and Design.
Description: 3rd edition. | New York : Fairchild Books, 2020.
Identifiers: LCCN 2019027321 | ISBN 9781501326714 (paperback) | ISBN
    9781501326721 (pdf)
Subjects: LCSH: Architectural drawing—Technique. | Interior decoration—Designs
    and plans.
Classification: LCC NA2708 .K56 2020 | DDC 720.28/4—dc23
LC record available at https://lccn.loc.gov/2019027321

ISBN: PB: 978-1-5013-2671-4
      ePDF: 978-1-5013-2672-1
      ePUB: 978-1-5013-2673-8

Typeset by Lachina Creative, Inc.
Printed and bound in the United States of America

To find out more about our authors and books visit www.fairchildbooks.com and
sign up for our newsletter.

Contents

Preface   x

CHAPTER one   Drafting Tools   2
CHAPTER two   Lettering   18
CHAPTER three   Architectural Elements Drawn in Plan View   30
CHAPTER four   Furniture and Plants Drawn in Plan View   44
CHAPTER five   Drawing Interior Materials in Plan View   71
CHAPTER six   Interior Elevations   87
CHAPTER seven   Section Drawings   99
CHAPTER eight   Electrical and Lighting Plans   105
CHAPTER nine   Kitchens and Baths   113
CHAPTER ten   Process Drawings   132
CHAPTER eleven   Custom Millwork   138
CHAPTER twelve   Quick Sketching   148
CHAPTER thirteen   Putting It All Together   160

Glossary   171

Extended Contents

Preface   x

    Changes in the new edition   x

    Acknowledgments   xi

CHAPTER one
Drafting Tools   2

Drafting Tools and How to Use Them   3

    Architect's Scale   3

    Six-Inch Architect's Scale   3

    Metric Scale   4

    T-Squares, Parallel Rules, and Drafting Arms   4

    Parallel Bar   5

    Drafting Arm   5

    Drafting Boards   6

    Drafting Tables   6

    Triangles   6

    Compass   8

    Templates   8

    Erasers   9

    Drafting Brushes   10

    Pencils   10

        Uses for Different Lead Weights   11

        Lead Holders   12

        Mechanical Pencils   12

        Wood Pencils   13

        Pencil Line Weight   13

        Types of Lines   14

    Drafting Vellum   15

    Keeping Your Tools Clean   15

    Pens   15

Tools and Tips   16

    Erasing Shield   16

    Sanding Block   16

    Kneaded Erasers   17

CHAPTER two
Lettering 18

Universal Notes on Lettering   19
Basic Block   20
      Upper   21
      Lower   21
      More Variations   22
      Still More Variations   23
      And More   24
Bold Lettering   25
      Bold Numbers   26
Using a Lettering Guide   27
Some Yes's   28
Some No's   29

CHAPTER three
**Architectural Elements Drawn
in Plan View 30**

Drawing Windows   31
Walls   32
      Interior Design Walls   33
Drawing Doors   35
      Typical Door Placement   36
      French Doors   37
      Sliding Doors   37
      Bifold Doors   38
      Pocket Doors   39
      Another Pocket Door   39
      Additional Doors   40
Architectural Details   41
Stairs   43

CHAPTER four
**Furniture and Plants Drawn
in Plan View 44**

Residential Furnishings   45
Chairs   45
      More Square Chairs   46
      Smaller Square Chairs   47
      Club Chair/Office Chair   48
      Chair Variation   49
      Drawing Sofas   50
      Sofa Variety   51
      More Sofas   52
      And More Sofa Styles   53
Drawing Tables with Chairs   54
Other Tables with Chairs   55
Drawing Beds   56
      Bed Design Ideas   57
Additional Furniture   58
Commercial Furnishings   59
      Office Furniture   59
      More Office Furniture   60
      Filing Cabinets   61
      Reception Desks   61
Plants in Plan View   62
      Plants   63
      More Plant Designs   64
      Plant Variations   65
      More Plant Variations   66
      And More   67
General Notes on Furniture Layout   68
Example Floor Plans with Clearances   69
      Living Room Conversation Area   69
      Dining or Conference Room   70
      Typical Office   70

CHAPTER **five**
Drawing Interior Materials in Plan View   71

Tile Flooring   72
More Tile Flooring   73
Additional Tile Flooring   74
Granite and Concrete   75
Flooring and Paving   76
    Wood Flooring   77
    Old World Wood Flooring   78
    More Wood Flooring   79
    Fun Wood Flooring   80
    Carpeting   81
    Area Rugs   82
    Area Rug Ideas   83
    Simpler Area Rugs   83
    Some Fun Area Rugs   84
    Flooring Detail—Foyer   85
    Example Plan with Flooring   86

CHAPTER **six**
Interior Elevations   87

Drawing Elevations   88
Furniture in Elevation   89
Drawing Items Sitting at an Angle in a Room   90
Drawing Windows   91
    Windows   92
    Draperies Outside View   92
    More Windows Looking Out   93
    Window Coverings   94
    Draperies   95

One Wall, Different Styles   96
Elevation of Room with Vaulted Ceiling   97
Elevation with Sloped Ceiling   97
Line Weight in Elevation   98

CHAPTER **seven**
Section Drawings   99

Building Section   101
Definition by Line Weight   102
Typical Section of Cabinet   103
Section of Flooring Transition   104
Section of Ceiling Soffit Detail   104

CHAPTER **eight**
Electrical and Lighting Plans   105

Switch Symbols   107
Receptacle Symbols   107
Lighting Symbols   108
Example Electric Plan   110
Example Reflected Ceiling Plan   111
Example Commercial RCP   112

CHAPTER **nine**
Kitchens and Baths   113

Kitchens   114
    The L-Shaped Kitchen   114
    Corridor Kitchens   115

U-Shaped Kitchen 116
One-Wall Kitchen 116
Height Requirements 117
Space Requirements 117
Standard Sizes 118
Standard Heights—Cabinets 118
Planning for a Barrier Free Kitchen 119
Kitchen Appliances 120
Example Kitchen Plan 122
Kitchen Elevations 123
Baths/Restrooms 125
Typical Bath Layouts 125
Bathrooms 127
More Tub and Shower Techniques 128
Planning for a Barrier Free Restroom 129
Example Master Bath 130
Typical Commercial Restroom 131

CHAPTER ten
Process Drawings 132

Bubble to Block Diagramming to Final Plan 133
Bubble to Block Diagramming 134
Pediatric Office Space Plan 135
Bubble to Block Diagramming #2 136
Office Space Plan #2 137

CHAPTER eleven
Custom Millwork 138

Shop Drawings 139
Conventional Flush Construction
with Face Frame 139

Flush Overlay Construction 140
Reveal Overlay Construction 141
Typical Joinery 142
Paneled Door Details 143
Custom Millwork 144

CHAPTER twelve
Quick Sketching 148

Pencil Sketches 150
Quick Elevation—Ink 152
Concept Development Sketching 153
Quick Elevation—Ink and Pencil 156
Loose Ideation Sketching—
Ink and Marker 157

CHAPTER thirteen
Putting It All Together 160

Title Blocks 163
Example Cover/Index Sheet 164
Example Typical Plan Sheet 165
References 166
Receptacle Symbols 167
Switch Symbols 168
Lighting—RCP Symbols 169

Glossary 171

Preface

As our profession evolves with technology, it is still important to develop hand drafting and sketching skills. Hand drafting will provide you with the ability to design with a sense of scale and communicate your ideas graphically. The ability to use hand sketching to scale will allow you to ideate quickly and solve problems of space planning and detail on the job site or during a client meeting. It will also help you consider human factors in your design, as you will have a better sense of scale in relation to the human anthropometric data. Thus, it is my opinion that though most firms and interior designers are moving toward the use of computer programs such as AutoCAD and Revit, it is still critical that you have the hand drafting and sketching skills necessary for success as an interior designer.

Changes in the new edition

Hand drafting is a learned skill that can be further developed with practice. Examples of different techniques are included in this edition. The new edition still focuses on 2D drawings but also adds ideas and examples that can be used in both residential and commercial interior design.

- This new edition explains how to use a lettering guide to easily improve your hand lettering skills.
- A discussion of using a metric scale and a conversion chart is included.
- Architectural Elements drawn in plan view are expanded upon, including ADA push/pull clearances at doors, and stairs.
- Furniture drawn in floor plans has more focus on commercial spaces, including examples with filing, reception desks, office layouts, and appropriate clearances.
- Drawing elevations and sections has been expanded to include more complex spaces with vaulted ceilings and furniture sitting at an angle in the room.

- Section drawing of details such as flooring, ceiling, and cabinets has been included in this edition.
- The kitchen and bath section includes planning for ADA (wheelchair-bound individuals and aging in place). Commercial restrooms are also covered.
- Space planning and using quick sketching to ideate using bubble and block diagramming have been added to this edition with examples of the process on completed floor plans.
- A chapter dedicated to drawings used for custom millwork has been added to this edition.
- A final chapter on putting it all together covers title blocks, sheet layout, index of drawings, and symbol legends.
- New example drawings are included throughout the book. As a student you can never look at enough examples to gain knowledge and ideas to improve your work.

Acknowledgments

Working on the revisions and drawings for the third edition of this book has been a wonderful experience. I would like to thank Bloomsbury for giving me this opportunity. In addition, I would like to thank my Seminole State College of Florida colleagues for their encouragement and support in this endeavor. My husband has been great throughout the process. While I was drawing through the weekends, he has been there to provide kind words and food. Lastly, I would like to thank my family for all they have done throughout my life. Without them, I would not be the person I am. It is an immense pleasure to share my knowledge and skills with students. It has been my life's mission, and this book is just another way that I can help students beyond the colleges and universities where I have taught.

Hand Drafting
for INTERIOR DESIGN

CHAPTER ONE

Drafting Tools

s interior designers, we need to be able to transform the creative ideas and plans in our minds into reality. In order to do this, we have to be able to effectively communicate those ideas and plans to others. Using the "tools of the trade" described in this chapter, interior designers can bring their wonderful ideas to the rest of the world by drafting them by hand on paper.

DRAFTING TOOLS AND HOW TO USE THEM

The first step in the process is learning which tools you need to have in order to get started. If you buy good tools in the beginning, they will last a lifetime. In this chapter, you will learn about the "tools of the trade" for drafting, including the pencils and proper pencil weights used for hand drafting in contemporary design.

Tools of the trade include:

1. Architect's scale
2. T-square, parallel rule, or drafting machine
3. Drafting board
4. Triangles
5. Compass
6. Templates
7. Erasers
8. Drafting brush
9. Pencils—wood or mechanical
10. Pens—Rapidiograph, Micron, Staedtler, Sharpie
11. Tracing vellum
12. Sanding block
13. Kneaded eraser

Architect's Scale

An architect's scale is used to accurately measure and scale a drawing in feet and inches. The major divisions are $1/32$, $1/16$, $1/8$, $3/16$, $1/4$, $3/8$, $1/2$, $3/4$, 1, $1\frac{1}{2}$, and 3. Each one of these divisions represents one foot on the scale in that scale size. For example, in the $1/4$-inch scale, one quarter of an inch on the scale represents one foot. When you use the scale, begin counting off the feet at the 0 point. The inches are scaled on the other side of the 0 point. Generally, residential plans are drawn in $1/4$-inch scale, and commercial plans are drawn in $1/8$-inch scale.

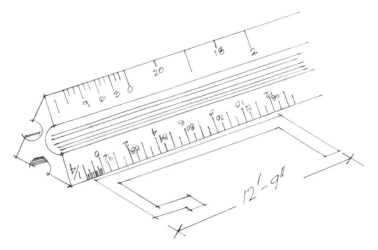

NOTE *The scale only looks complicated; it actually is very simple once you start using it. I like to take a permanent marker and mark the $1/4$-inch scale so that I can see more easily which side of the scale I'm using when working.*

Six-Inch Architect's Scale

The 6-inch architect's scale is a small, simple scale to use. I find it great to use when laying out floor plans. Using this smaller size scale takes away the confusion of flipping the larger scale.

Metric Scale

Most manufacturers and firms in the United States are still using the imperial numbering system shown in the previous architect scales. You may find that you have an occasion to use the metric system. You can purchase metric scales and tape measures. You can also find metric conversion calculators online. If you need to provide only some measurements in metric, you can use the chart below for conversion from feet and inches to meters and centimeters.

Metric Conversion Table

Original Measurement	Multiply by	To Obtain
Inches	2.54	Centimeters (cm)
Feet	0.3048	Meters (m)
Square Feet	0.0929	Square meters (m²)

T-Squares, Parallel Rules, and Drafting Arms

T-squares come in different lengths, from 18 inches to 48 inches. Pick the one that is appropriate to the board or table you are using to draft. T-squares are fairly inexpensive and come in either metal or wood with a see-through plastic edge. They need to be held in place while you are drawing, because the end farthest from the angle may move a bit if you do not hold it. The T-square is portable, which makes it convenient for design students.

NOTE *If your drafting board is a little cracked on the edge, line up your paper with the edge of the board and your drawing will be straight.*

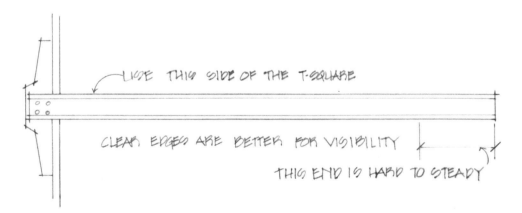

USE THIS SIDE OF THE T-SQUARE

CLEAR EDGES ARE BETTER FOR VISIBILITY

THIS END IS HARD TO STEADY

Parallel Bar

Because they are easier to keep in place, the parallel bar (also called the parallel rule) and the drafting arm can be used in place of a T-square. The parallel bar is attached to a drafting board with a system of pulleys and cables, allowing the straight edge to move up and down the board in a parallel manner. It is always parallel to the top of the board. The parallel rule is easy to use, and it allows the person drafting to move the bar up and down and draft in a faster manner than using the T-square. Like T-squares, parallel rules also are available in a variety of lengths from 30 inches to 60 inches.

Rollers permit the parallel rule to move easily across the drafting surface. Clear acrylic edges make it easy to see the lines you have drawn.

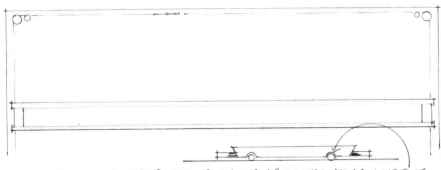

ROLLERS KEEP THE RULE UP FROM DRAWING SURFACE

Drafting Arm

Drafting arms, also called drafting machines, combine the best of the T-square and the parallel rule. A drafting arm is attached to your drafting board or table. It has built-in scales on the horizontal and vertical blades, so you do not have to have a separate architect's scale for measuring. Drafting machines are made for left- and right-handed people. You can rotate the head by pressing and releasing the lock and use the arm at angles, similar to how a triangle is used.

There are two types of drafting arms:

1 The arm type has two arms that rotate in the middle, extended from an arm that is clamped to the top of your board or table.

2 The track type is attached to the board at the top of the board with a horizontal bar across the top with a vertical track attached that slides to the left and right.

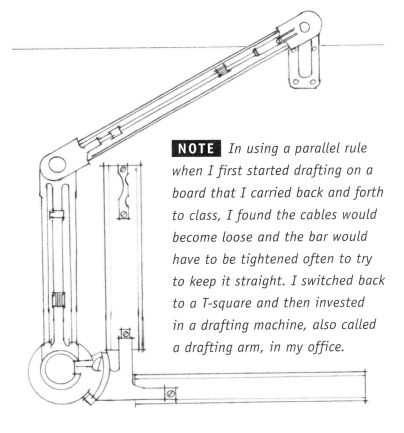

NOTE *In using a parallel rule when I first started drafting on a board that I carried back and forth to class, I found the cables would become loose and the bar would have to be tightened often to try to keep it straight. I switched back to a T-square and then invested in a drafting machine, also called a drafting arm, in my office.*

Drafting Boards

Drafting boards come in a wide variety of shapes and sizes. Schools often suggest that students have a lightweight board to carry back and forth to class. At home, a drafting table or drafting stand is a better solution. A drafting stand has an adjustable top, so that you can work at an angle comfortable for you. Search the Internet and you likely will find the size you want.

NOTE *I like to cover the top of my drafting table with Borco™ (Trademark registered with Safco Products Co., Minneapolis, Minnesota). It is a vinyl cover that is stain-resistant, easy on the eyes, and "self-healing" for your pencil lines.*

Drafting Tables

Drafting tables are also available in a wide variety of sizes, materials, and shapes. They usually have a shallow drawer on one side. Regardless of whether you have a drafting table or a drafting board, I recommend that you cover it with a Borco or VYCO surface. This gives a nice surface that improves line quality.

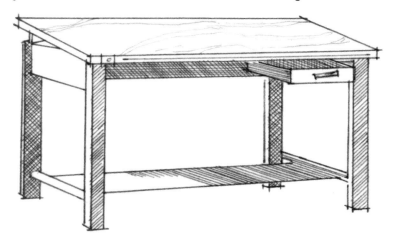

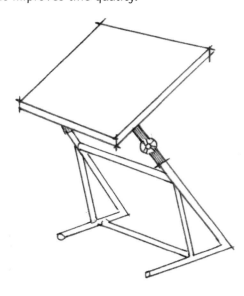

Triangles

Triangles generally are made out of clear, scratch-resistant acrylic and provide a clear, undistorted view of your drawing. Triangles come in a variety of sizes: 45/90-degree, 30/60-degree, and, my favorite, the adjustable triangle, which can adjust from 0 to 45 degrees.

NOTE *The size of the triangle is determined by the length of the longest side of the right angle.*

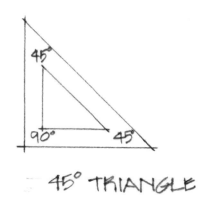

45° TRIANGLE

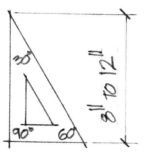

30°–60° TRIANGLE

The adjustable triangle is held in place by a thumbscrew with a movable arm. Line up the scales in the middle to make different angles. The adjustable triangle is convenient for a variety of sloping lines, such as angled furniture or stairs.

Large triangles are great for drawing long vertical lines perpendicular to the edge of the T-square. Small triangles are perfect for lettering or for the detailed hatch marks in drawings.

You can combine triangles to draw longer lines or parallel lines. You also can combine triangles to draw different angles, but I find the adjustable triangle works best for this.

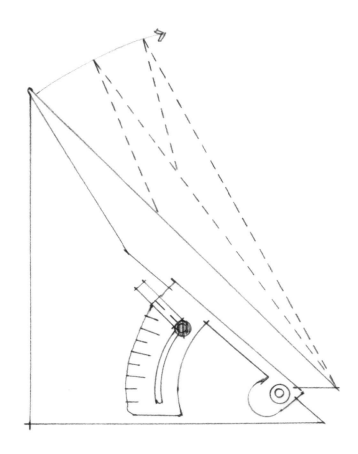

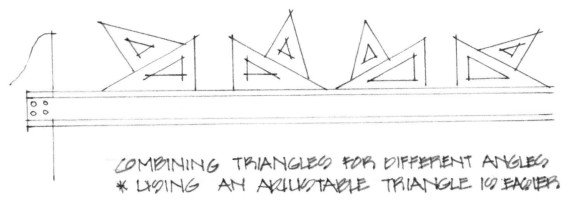

COMBINING TRIANGLES FOR DIFFERENT ANGLES
* USING AN ADJUSTABLE TRIANGLE IS EASIER

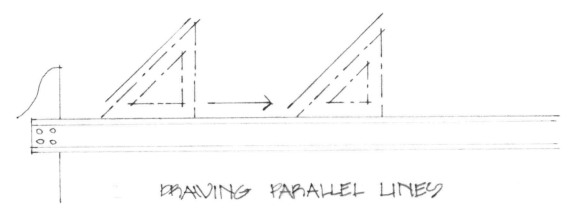

DRAWING PARALLEL LINES

Compass

Compasses are needed in order to draw large circles. Circle templates work best for smaller circles because you have more control of your lead pressure. It can be difficult to apply even pressure using a compass. A chisel point for your compass pencil works best in an F lead. An H lead or harder will produce too light a line.

An extension arm can be added for larger circles.

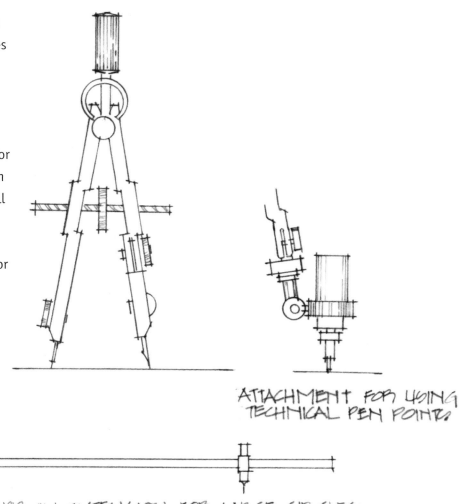

ATTACHMENT FOR USING
TECHNICAL PEN POINTS

ADD AN EXTENSION FOR LARGE CIRCLES

Templates

Templates, made of acrylic with cutouts of predetermined shapes, are useful when beginning your layouts. Circle templates, for example, have circles of graduated sizes. They can be used for door swings, tables, artwork, and laying out plants, as well as a variety of other elements in drawings. There are templates for kitchen equipment, bath equipment, living room furniture,

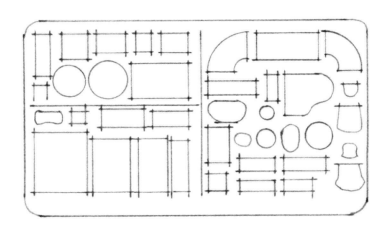

bedroom furniture, office furniture, and ellipses. Templates are available in ⅛-inch scale and ¼-inch scale for architectural drawings. Many beginning design students go no further in the drawing process than using templates to show furniture and equipment in the floor plan. Templates are just the beginning. Templates should be used as a guide to help place furniture in the floor plan. A designer should then draw the furniture and the details using the techniques illustrated in this book, using beautiful and delicate hand drafting.

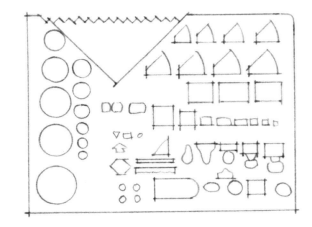

Erasers

One of the wonderful advantages of pencil drafting is being able to erase mistakes. One of the disadvantages of pencil drafting is that not all lines can be easily erased. Erasers come in a variety of shapes and sizes. Try different ones to see what works best for your style.

A good electric eraser could be your new best friend. Battery-operated erasers and rechargeable erasers are also available.

Kneaded erasers work great in large areas.

Pink Pearl and White Vinyl erasers are available in art supply and drafting supply stores. I prefer the White Vinyl eraser. When it becomes dirty, you can just erase on a clean sheet of paper to remove the residual graphite.

The erasing shield may be a small piece of equipment, but it can play a big role in your design drawing process. The erasing shield is a small rectangle of metal with various shaped holes, intended to be placed over your drawing in progress to isolate and eliminate your mistakes. It is effective in protecting your drawing while using an electric eraser.

ELECTRIC ERASER

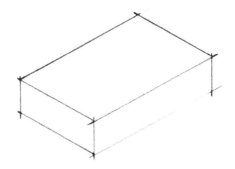

PINK PEARL OR WHITE VINYL ERASERS

Drafting Brushes

Keeping the surface of your drawing clean is of the utmost importance. Every time you erase, you need to use your drafting brush to clean off the extra graphite. I find the softer the brush, the easier it is to keep clean.

Drafting powder can be used as a protective coating over drawings while drafting. But drafting powder can be tricky, in that if you use too much, your lines may skip. It can be safer and easier to put a piece of tracing paper over the part you have completed.

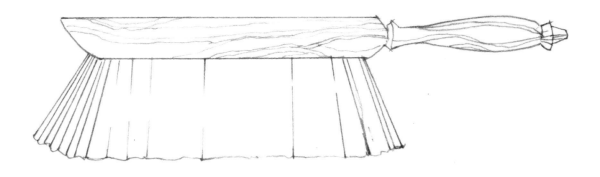

Pencils

There are many types of drafting pencils that can successfully be used for drafting.
Pencil weights range from 9H to 6B, as shown on the chart below.

Hard								Medium						Soft
9H	8H	6H	4H	3H	2H	H	F	HB	B	2B	3B	4B	5B	6B

Pencils used for design drafting are usually 4H to B.
Anything harder will tear the vellum and anything softer will smudge too easily.

Uses for Different Lead Weights

4H

4H lead is hard and dense and great for initial layout of drawings where you are going to fill in later with more detail. The lines will be light and hard to read and not reproduce well in finished drawings. People who have a "heavy hand" can carefully use this lead for details. If it is applied too intensely, it will tear the vellum or leave marks on your drafting table.

2H

2H lead is great for filling in details in a drawing. It is suitable for finished drawings, but only if used with some pressure. If too light pressure is used, it will not show up; too much pressure and you can tear the vellum. Use this lead weight to draw detail in furniture and to poché (fill in) the walls in floor plans. If drawn with a heavy hand, 2H is difficult to erase.

H

H lead pencil is superb for the detail lines in drawings. H can be used to darken windows or mirrors, as will be shown in upcoming chapters. It also can be used to fill in walls, if you do not have a heavy hand, and draw in details on area rugs, plants, or any other object of interest.

F

F lead pencil is my favorite pencil. You can use it to make the darkest lines without much smudging, if carefully applied. Use the F pencil for lettering, walls, and outside lines on furniture in finished drawings.

HB

HB was used more when everything was blue printed, as it can show up as quite dark. It can be used for dense line-work or hand lettering, but it will also easily smudge so should not be used without great care.

B

B lead is very soft and can make impressive dark lines. It is better used for sketching and drawing than drafting.

Lead Holders

Lead holders use 2 mm leads that can be drawn out or pulled
back by the push-button on the end controlling the length
of the lead. The lead can be contracted when not in use. The
different lead weights can be used in any lead holder. The
point of the lead will be sharpened with a lead pointer.

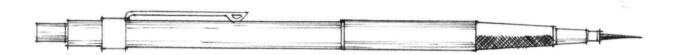

Mechanical Pencils

Mechanical pencils use 0.3 mm, 0.5 mm, 0.7 mm, and 0.9 mm leads:

- 0.3 mm are for fine lines, but they do break easily.
- 0.5 mm are used most often as they are hardier.
- 0.7 mm and 0.9 mm are better for sketching and lettering.

Mechanical pencils work with the same push-button mechanism as lead
holders. The mechanical pencils hold thin leads that do not need to
be sharpened. I feel that mechanical pencils do not allow for as much
control of your lines, so I prefer to use lead holders.

Wood Pencils

Wood pencils have always been my choice for drafting. I feel that by actually touching the pencil, you are more in touch with your drafting. There are many brands of wood pencils available; try several different ones to see which is most comfortable in your hand and produces the best lines for you. For example, Mars Staedtler Lumograph has been my brand of preference for many years. You do have to sharpen your pencil every few strokes. In the past it was recommended to sharpen to a long (¾") thin point and then use a lead pointer or sandpaper to refine the point even more. I find a good electric pencil sharpener works best.

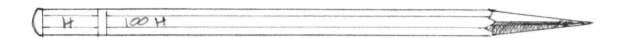

Of course, it is a personal preference as to which style of pencil you use for your drafted drawings. Used correctly, all three—wood, mechanical, or lead holder—can produce beautiful quality in line drawings. Try out each style and see what feels best to you personally. In addition to the pencil type, you need to work with the lead weight that works best for you. For instance, if you have a heavy hand, you will find harder leads (4H, 2H, H) a better choice to create crisp line quality. If you have oily hands, you will find that harder leads smudge less. If you have a light touch and dry hands, you may find that softer leads (F, HB, B) are a better choice. With practice and experimentation, you will find what works best for you to create nice, crisp, dark line quality in the correct line weight.

NOTE *Be sure to rotate your pencil between your thumb and forefinger as you are drafting long lines, and apply an even and steady pressure. It will give you a cleaner and neater line without the fuzzy lines that most beginning drafting students always have. And be sure to sharpen your pencil at least twice as often as you think you should.*

Pencil Line Weight

Lines and their use are the essence of drafting. It is important to know what different lines represent in the art of drafting. If you understand the use of the different lines, you will have an easier time drawing all your plans and anyone reading them should be able to understand.

All lines should be uniformly dense, not fuzzy, so they are easier to read and will reproduce the same. Each pencil lead produces a slightly different weight of line. Pencils can vary from one brand to the next within the same pencil weight. For example, a Berol Turquoise H pencil might be slightly different than a Mars Staedtler Lumograph H pencil.

Types of Lines

Solid lines define the form of objects, such as the outside line of a floor plan. The darker the line, the more the space is defined.

- Dashed lines indicate essentials hidden from view. The upper cabinets in a kitchen would be shown this way.
- Centerlines, shown by long lines, then short dashes or long dots, show the axis.
- Grid lines drawn with a light hand in H or 2H pencil are great for setting up tile and wood floors.

SOLID OUTSIDE LINE

DETAIL LINE

SUPPLEMENTARY DETAILS

DASHED LINES

CENTER LINE

GRID LINES

MAJOR LINES
F OR H

SECONDARY LINES
H OR 2H

GRID OR LAYOUT LINES
H, 2H, OR 4H

Drafting Vellum

Drafting vellum is a high-quality transparent paper that is easily drawn on with pencils and from which drawings can be erased without great difficulty. Reproductions can be made from pencil drawings on drafting vellum. The paper also takes ink well, without bleeding.

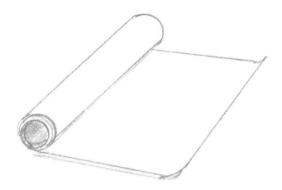

DRAFTING VELLUM CAN BE PURCHASED IN ROLLS OR SHEETS.

Keeping Your Tools Clean

When drafting with pencil, you will get a buildup of graphite and oil from your hands on your tools. In order to keep your drawings neat and free of smudges, it is crucial to keep your tools clean. You can use alcohol wipes to clean your tools. I also recommend keeping your handheld sharpener in a separate bag from the rest of your tools. This will prevent the graphite dust from spilling on your other tools and drawings. You can keep some packets of alcohol wipes with your supplies; they will come in handy. Make sure the tools have air dried before you use them again.

Pens

The majority of the time you will use pencil for hand drafting of process work and construction drawings. Many will use pens for presentation drawings. Rapidiograph, Staedtler, and Micron pens are all available with different mm points. This allows you to use .03, .05, .07, and .09 to achieve different line weights in your drawings.

TOOLS AND TIPS

There are several tools that I personally use on a daily basis to make my drafting quicker, neater, and more efficient. My favorites of these tools are described below.

Erasing Shield

One of the puzzles of beginning drafting is the erasing shield, an item of which beginning drafters never see the value. Erasing shields come in various sizes and shapes, are invaluable once you know how to use them, and are very simple! The thin, stainless steel shields effectively protect the drawing surface while you use the electric eraser to erase defined areas. I love it, because you can easily and effectively correct your own mistakes.

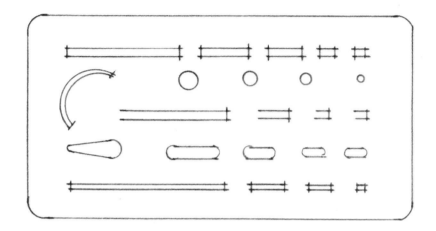

Sanding Block

The sanding block is a piece of wood with sandpaper sheets stapled to the end. It is used to obtain a tapered, conical point on your pencil or angle the end of the point for lettering. The point of your pencil, whether mechanical or lead holder or wood, makes the difference in drawing and particularly in lettering—the point of your pencil needs to be angled to do excellent lettering.

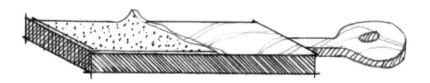

Do not let your pencil get too dull, or you will have fuzzy line quality. You can use the sanding block between sharpening to keep a very sharp point.

 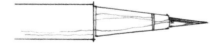 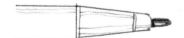

Kneaded Erasers

My favorite eraser is a
Kneaded Rubber Eraser by
Banford. To clean it, you
have to pull and stretch.
Kneaded erasers are great
for cleaning surfaces.

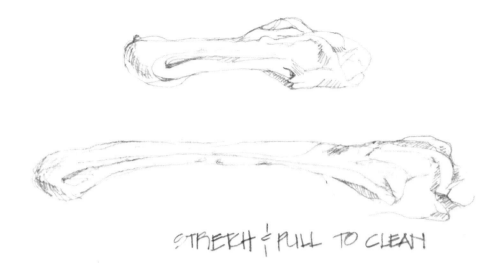

STRECH & PULL TO CLEAN

. . . And a trick about rolling your drawings.

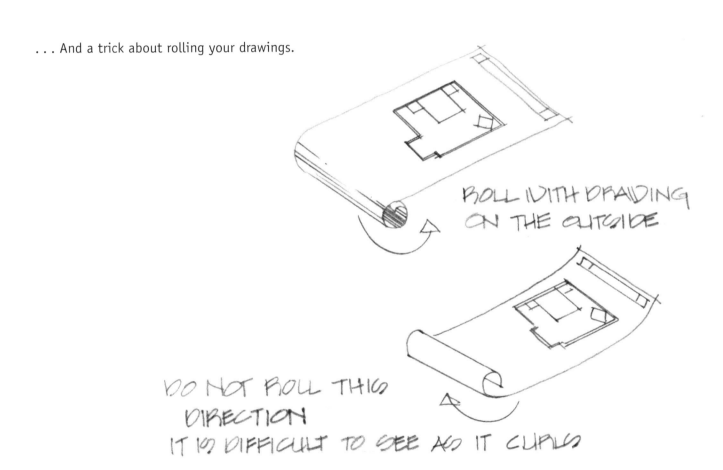

ROLL WITH DRAWING
ON THE OUTSIDE

DO NOT ROLL THIS
DIRECTION
IT IS DIFFICULT TO SEE AS IT CURLS

CHAPTER two

Lettering

here are entire books written solely on lettering. Good lettering can make the difference between a merely acceptable presentation and an impressive one. Professional lettering styles should be taught and practiced from the beginning of the study of interior design. There is a range of lettering styles that are suitable to use in conjunction with hand drafting. Well-executed and artistically drawn lettering can mean gaining entrée to the professional office of your preference.

UNIVERSAL NOTES ON LETTERING

This chapter will show you the basics of good lettering and then some variety of that lettering. We should begin with some universal notes on lettering:

- Lettering should be all uppercase (caps).
- Lettering should always be drawn with a top and bottom guideline for uniformity.
  - A well-sharpened 4H pencil works well for guidelines because it is a hard pencil and can make a very thin line.
  - Guidelines never need be erased; they become part of the design.
- One-eighth-inch lettering is considered standard.
- Space between lines should also be $\frac{1}{8}$ of an inch.
- Use a lettering guide or small triangle for all vertical lines on lettering.
- Your freehand lettering will improve with practice.
- Curvy or playful lettering is inappropriate.
- Use an Ames Lettering guide to set guidelines.
- One-quarter-inch or block lettering is used in title blocks for client description.
- It is accepted practice in lettering to have the vertical stroke thin and the horizontal thicker. This is explained in more detail later in this chapter.

Finding your own lettering style is fun, as you try many different styles within the suitable range until you find one that works well for you. This chapter begins by illustrating basic block lettering. If you learn basic block lettering in the beginning, you can then adapt and change it to your style or to the style of the design firm where you work. Lettering is like anything else: if you understand how it works first, you can make it your own later.

BASIC BLOCK

ABCDEFGHIJKLMNO
PQRSTUVWXYZ

ALL THE LETTERS ARE BASICALLY SQUARE AND THE SAME SIZE. W AND M ARE A LITTLE WIDER.

FROM THIS BASIC FORMAT YOU CAN ADD WHAT I CALL "PERSONALITY."

NOTE:

DO NOT ADD TAILS TO I OR J IN A SIMPLE BLOCK

I J

OR ANY ARCHITECTURAL LETTERING.

PERSONALITY MIGHT BE MOVING THE CENTER LINE UP OR DOWN.

FORM EVER FOLLOWS FUNCTION

FORM EVER FOLLOWS FUNCTION.
LOUIS HENRY SULLIVAN

DO NOT VARY WITHIN EACH STYLE.
UPPER VERSUS LOWER

UPPER
A B C D E F G H I J K L M N O
P Q R S T U V W X Y Z
NOTE THE B, K, P, R, AND S CENTER LINE.

LOWER
A B C D E F G H I J K L M N
O P Q R S T U V W X Y Z
NOTE THE SAME LETTERS WITH LOWER.

ANOTHER WAY TO CHANGE THE BASIC BLOCK
IS MAKE THE HORIZONTAL LINES AT A SLANT.

A B C D E F G H I J K L M N O
P Q R S T U V W X Y Z

NOTES
- KEEP THE ANGLE OF THE SLANT CONSISTENT
- THE Z DOES NOT ANGLE Z TOO CUTE
- VERTICAL LINES SHOULD TOUCH GUIDELINES

ALL ART IS BUT IMITATION
OF NATURE.
LUCIUS ANNAEUS SENECA

MORE VARIATIONS

SLANTING THE LETTERS GIVES A DIFFERENT LOOK. KEEPING THE ANGLE THE SAME IS THE DIFFICULT PART.

ANOTHER VERSION MAKES THE STRAIGHT LINE LETTERS THIN AND THE ROUND LETTERS WIDE. THE ROUND LETTERS CAN BE A BIT LARGER.

A B C D E F G H I J K L M N O P Q R S T U V W X Y Z

FRANK LLOYD WRIGHT USED WIDE SPACING AND NARROW STRAIGHT LINES AND WIDE ROUND LETTERS SIMILAR TO ABOVE.

HE ALSO DESIGNED ART DECO FONTS A B C D E F G H I J K L M N O P Q R S T U V W X Y Z

DIANA'S STYLE

MY PERSONAL STYLE IS A COMBINATION OF SEVERAL STYLES.

A B C D E F G H I J K L M N O P Q R S T U V W X Y Z

MORE VARIATIONS
ABCDEFGHIJKLMNOPQRS
TUVWXYZ 1234567890

+ NOTE IT DOES NOT TAKE MUCH TO CHANGE A STYLE.

STUDENTS OFTEN LIKE TO ADD LOTS OF CURVES
ABCDEFGHIJKLMNOPQRST
UVWXYZ 1234567890

THIS IS NOT A STYLE I RECOMMEND!

STUDENTS OFTEN DESIGN ALPHABETS WITH A
WIDE RANGE OF DEVIATION. IN DESIGNING
YOUR LETTERING BE SURE ALL YOUR LETTERS ARE
COHESIVE.

HERE IS ANOTHER STYLE YOU
MIGHT WANT TO ADAPT TO USE.

ABCDEFGHIJKMNOPQRS
TUVWXYZ 123456789

SOME MERELY CHANGE THE LOOK BY EXTENDING
AN OCCASIONAL LETTER, WHICH GIVES YOU A WHOLE
NEW LOOK.

YOU CAN HAVE FUN
WITH LETTERING.

AND MORE

ABCDEFGHIJKLMNOPQRSTUVWXYZ
1234567890
LETTERING STYLE

ABCDEFGHIJKLMNOPQRSTUVWX
YZ   1234567
LETTERING STYLE
THIS IS A FUN AND DIFFERENT
STYLE.

HAVE FUN
WITH
YOUR STYLE.

BOLD LETTERING

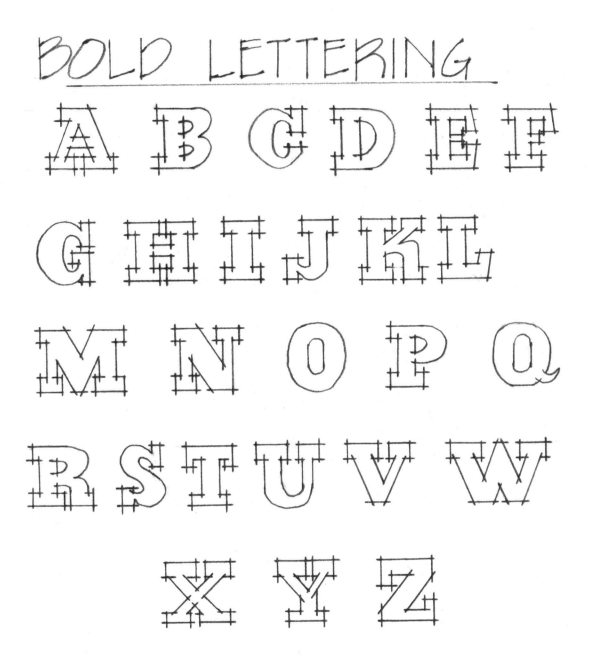

THE LETTERING SHOWN ABOVE CAN BE USED FOR
THE NAME OF THE PROJECT IN A TITLE BLOCK.
IT IS BEST TO TRACE LETTERS FORMING THE
NAME ON A SEPARATE PRACTICE SHEET FIRST.

BOLD NUMBERS

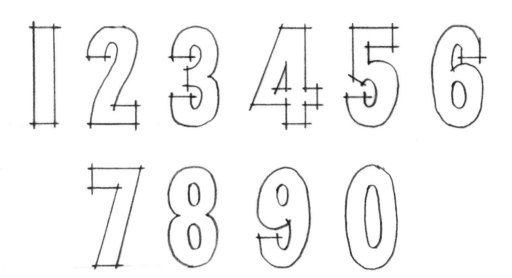

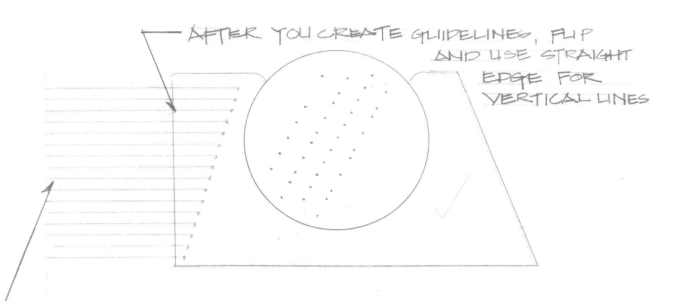

AFTER YOU CREATE GUIDELINES, FLIP AND USE STRAIGHT EDGE FOR VERTICAL LINES

USING A LETTERING GUIDE HELPS YOU CREATE GUIDELINES ACCURATELY AND QUICKLY. SIMPLY USE A HARD LEAD (2H, 4H) AND USE THE HOLES TO GUIDE YOUR PENCIL AS SHOWN ABOVE.

NOW THAT YOU HAVE SEEN SOME EXAMPLES AND ARE FAMILIAR WITH THE LETTERING GUIDE LET'S GET STARTED.

☑ CREATE GUIDELINES @ 1/8"

☑ PRACTICE THESE SIX LINES & SHAPES
| | | | | | | | | | | VERTICAL LINES - USE STRAIGHT EDGE, (FLIP THE GUIDE)
≡ ≡ ≡ ≡ ≡ HORIZONTAL LINES - SLANT MAY VARY, BUT BE CONSISTENT
C C C))) THESE SHAPES CAN ALSO VARY WITH STYLES OF LETTERING
/ / / / / / / \ \ \ \ \ THESE DIAGONAL LINES ROUND OUT THE SHAPES YOU WILL USE FOR LETTERING
☑ USE A STYLE THAT IS COMFORTABLE AND NATURAL TO YOUR HAND. PRACTICE...

SOME YES's

- ALWAYS DRAW THE VERTICAL LINES FIRST WITH A CHISEL POINT
- THEN DRAW THE HORIZONTAL LINES WITH THE "FAT" PART OF THE CHISEL

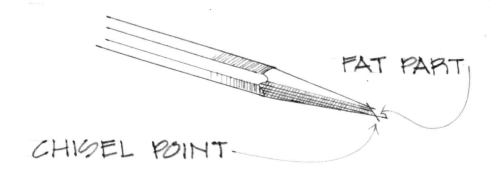

FAT PART

CHISEL POINT

- ADD EMPHASIS (DARKEN WITH PRESSURE) TO THE BEGINNING AND END OF EVERY LINE

ESPECIALLY WITH YOUR LETTERING

A B C D E F G H I J K L M

OR LOOKING AT A LARGER VIEW

A B C D E

NOTE EMPHASIS

SOME NO's

IN LETTERING NO's CAN ONLY BE SHOWN BY EXAMPLE:

- DON'T MAKE YOUR LETTERING
  ## TOO WIDE

- OR   TOO NARROW AND CLOSE

- OR   TOO CLOSE.

- AND NOT TOO SLOPPY

- PLUS DON'T DO YOUR LETTERING
  TILL LAST. IT WILL SMUDGE

AND DON'T FORGET
TO PRACTICE !

CHAPTER three

Architectural Elements
Drawn in Plan View

indows, walls, doors, and other permanent structural fixtures such as fireplaces and stairs must be drawn on the floor plan in a uniform manner that is legible, simple, and easily understood. This chapter includes step-by-step illustrations of how to draw a selection of windows, walls, and doors generally used in interior design and construction.

As interior designers we often find ourselves designing the layouts for remodels, additions, and commercial interior space planning for our clients. Once the design is complete, we must always hire an engineer or knowledgeable contractor to make sure that load-bearing walls are not being affected and that the existing structure will be safe.

This is a very simple chapter, but it is very necessary to be precise.

DRAWING WINDOWS

WINDOWS ARE BEST DRAWN IN A SIMPLE MANNER.

FIXED WINDOWS

DRAW THE WALL FIRST USING "F" PENCIL.
A FIXED WINDOW IS DEPICTED WITH ONE LINE
IN THE CENTER USING PENCIL "H".

DOUBLE HUNG WINDOWS

DRAWN THE SAME AS FIXED WINDOWS WITH
TWO LINES DRAWN IN THE CENTER IN "H".

WINDOW WITH SILL

DRAWN AS ABOVE WITH EXTENDED SILL

BAY WINDOW

WALLS

WALLS ARE DRAWN A BIT SIMPLER IN AN INTERIOR DESIGN DRAWING THAN IN A SET OF ARCHITECTURAL DOCUMENTS.

WALLS ARE GENERALLY DRAWN AT 6 INCHES. PLUMBING WALLS ARE DRAWN AT 9 INCHES.

CONSTRUCTION WALLS

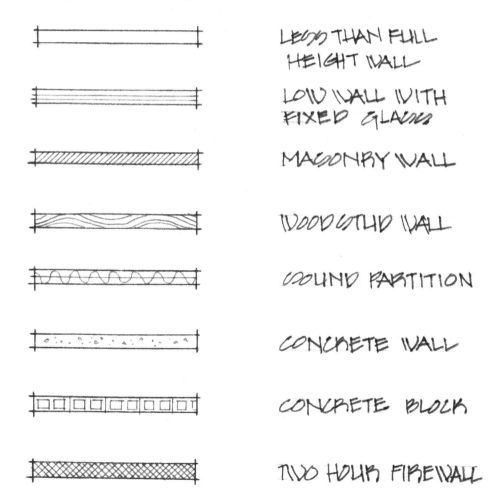

LESS THAN FULL HEIGHT WALL

LOW WALL WITH FIXED GLASS

MASONRY WALL

WOOD STUD WALL

SOUND PARTITION

CONCRETE WALL

CONCRETE BLOCK

TWO HOUR FIREWALL

INTERIOR DESIGN WALLS

DRAWINGS USED FOR PRESENTATION BY
INTERIOR DESIGNERS COMMONLY POCHE'
THE WALLS

POCHE' — LITERALLY MEANS 'POCKET' IN FRENCH.
IN INTERIOR DESIGN DRAWINGS WE
FILL IN THE POCKET OF THE WALLS
IN FLOOR PLANS FOR IMPROVED
READABILITY.

HOW TO POCHE'
DRAW THE WALL IN 'F' PENCIL.
FILL IN WITH FINE LINES IN 'H' OR '2H'.

YES —

DON'T MAKE THE LINES TOO DARK
OR TOO FAR APART.

NO —

SEE THE DIFFERENCE. THE FIRST
ONE DRAWN LOOKS MUCH BETTER.

DRAWING CORNERS

DRAW A 45° ANGLE
IN THE CORNER
VERY LIGHTLY.

DRAW LINES TO MEET
AT THE ANGLE.

MAKE EMPHASIS
AT BEGINNING & END.

POCHE' OF INTERIOR CORNERS

BUTT THE SHORTER
WALL OF POCHE' INTO
THE LONGER WALL.

ANOTHER STYLE OF POCHE'

THIS IS A FREER-LOOKING STYLE DONE FREE HAND.

TOTAL POCHE' FILL IN

THIS STYLE SEEMS TOO PLAIN OR BORING
TO ME PERSONALLY.

DRAWING DOORS

DRAW THE WALL VERY LIGHTLY IN 4H PENCIL.
MEASURE TO PLACE THE DOOR.

DRAW THE WALL WITH YOUR F PENCIL.

THE DOOR IS DRAWN THE SAME AS THE WIDTH OF
THE OPENING. IF THE DOOR IS 3'-0" WIDE, THE
DOOR IS DRAWN 3'-0" LONG.

THE DOOR IS DRAWN USING THE H PENCIL.
THE DOOR IS DRAWN AT 2" DEEP FITTING INSIDE
THE OPENING.

THE DOOR SWING IS DRAWN USING A CIRCLE
TEMPLATE WITH H PENCIL.

TYPICAL DOOR PLACEMENT

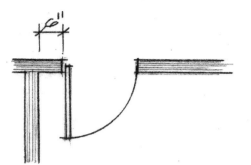

6"

TYPICALLY A DOOR IS PLACED IN THE CORNER OF A ROOM 6" FROM THE WALL.

DOOR SIZES CAN VARY FOR DIFFERENT FUNCTIONS. YOU SHOULD PLAN FOR THE FOLLOWING COMMON SIZES:

- ☑ 2'-8" (32") MINIMUM A.D.A. CLEARANCE
- ☑ 3'-0" (36") COMMONLY USED IN COMMERCIAL DESIGN. YOU SHOULD SPECIFY THIS SIZE FOR A WHEELCHAIR BOUND CLIENT.

A.D.A. (AMERICAN DISABILITIES ACT) STANDARDS AND GUIDELINES

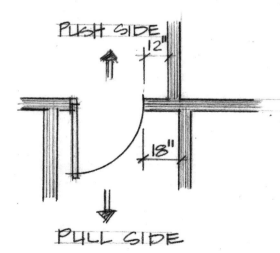

PUSH SIDE

12"

18"

PULL SIDE

WHEN LAYING OUT SPACES FOR COMMERCIAL DESIGN YOU MUST PROVIDE THESE PUSH/PULL CLEARANCES

FRENCH DOORS

FRENCH DOORS ARE DRAWN THE SAME AS SINGLE
DOORS. THE DOOR SWINGS MUST BE CENTERED

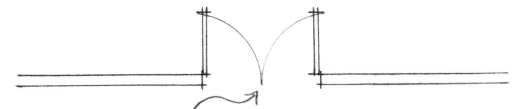

NOTE THAT THE SWING IS DRAWN TO THE
BOTTOM OF THE WALL.

* CROSS CORNERS AS SHOWN

SLIDING DOORS

ONCE AGAIN DRAW THE WALL AND MEASURE
THE DOOR OPENING. WALLS ARE GENERALLY
DRAWN AS 6" THICK.

DRAW THE CENTER FIRST.

DIVIDE IN HALF AND DRAW EACH SIDE OF THE DOOR.
TRY TO DRAW THEM BOTH AS EVENLY AS YOU CAN.

ANOTHER STYLE OF SLIDING DOORS

BIFOLD DOORS

BIFOLD DOORS CAN BE DRAWN IN SEVERAL DIFFERENT WAYS.

45 DEGREES
   THE DOORS ARE AT 45°

FIGURE THE WIDTH OF EACH DOOR AND DRAW IT THE PROPER SIZE.

12.5 DEGREES

THE IDEA IS THE SAME, BUT PRODUCES A DIF-FERENT LOOK.

ONE SIDE CLOSED

ACCORDION FOLDING

IDENTICAL TO BIFOLD DOORS WITH SHORTER SECTIONS

POCKET DOORS

THE OPENING IN THE WALL MUST BE THE SAME
DEPTH AS THE WIDTH OF THE DOOR.

1/4" = 1'-0"

DRAW THE WALL AND THE DOOR FIRST, THEN
ADD THE OPENING IN THE WALL FOR THE
DOOR TO GO INTO.

1/4" = 1'-0"

ANOTHER POCKET DOOR

POCKET DOORS CAN BE DRAWN IN MORE
THAN ONE MANNER.

ADDITIONAL DOORS

DOUBLE SWINGING DOORS GO BOTH DIRECTIONS.

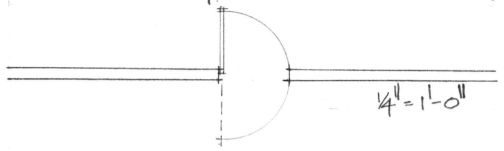

$\frac{1}{4}" = 1'-0"$

REVOLVING DOORS

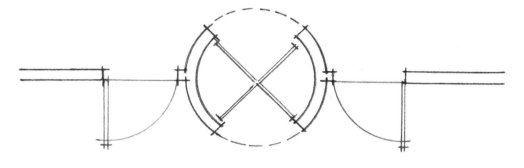

CASED OPENING

EXTERIOR DOOR

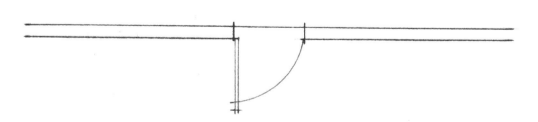

ARCHITECTURAL DETAILS

PLACING CLOTHING IN A CLOSET ADDS LIFE TO YOUR DRAWING. IT CAN BE DRAWN FREEHAND OR USING A TRIANGLE.

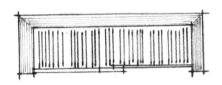

USING A TRIANGLE IS SIMPLE AND GIVES YOU A MORE CONTEMPORARY LOOK.

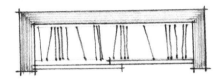

CLOTHES CAN BE DRAWN IN A SIMPLE MANNER IN A FREEHAND FORM.

DRAPERIES CAN BE SHOWN IN SEVERAL WAYS. USING GUIDELINES AND A CONNECTED U MAKE A REALISTIC LOOK.

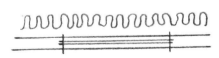

WIGGLY LINES DRAWN BETWEEN GUIDELINES

*NOTE: ALWAYS LEAVE 6" BETWEEN THE WINDOW & THE WALL.

ARCHITECTURAL DETAILS CONTINUED

 VERTICAL BLINDS ARE DRAWN WITH ANGLED LINES.

 VERTICAL BLINDS CAN BE DRAWN WITH A DOUBLE LINE.

 OR IN A VERY SIMPLE ANGLE.

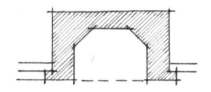 FIRE PLACES LOOK BEST FILLED WITH A 45-DEGREE LINE.

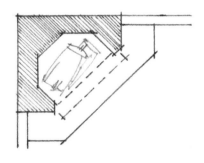 CORNER FIREPLACE WITH LOGS

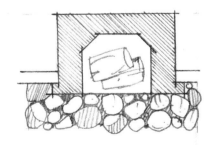 FIREPLACE WITH RIVER ROCK HEARTH

NOTE: THE FRONT OF THE RIVER ROCK IS DRAWN UNEVENLY JUST LIKE ROCK.

STAIRS

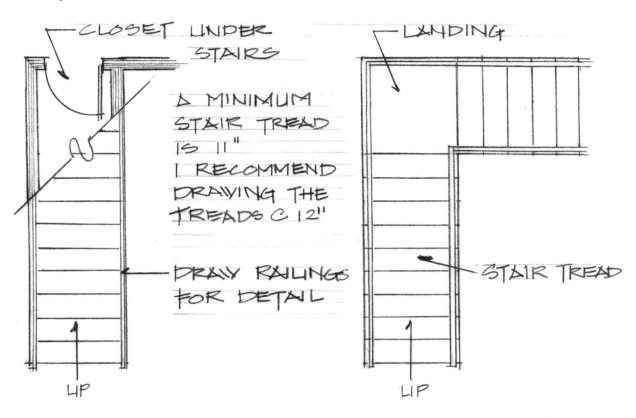

CLOSET UNDER STAIRS

△ MINIMUM STAIR TREAD IS 11"
I RECOMMEND DRAWING THE TREADS ⊂ 12"

DRAW RAILINGS FOR DETAIL

UP

LANDING

STAIR TREAD

UP

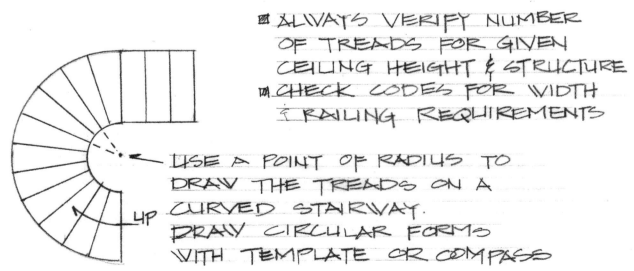

☑ ALWAYS VERIFY NUMBER OF TREADS FOR GIVEN CEILING HEIGHT & STRUCTURE
☑ CHECK CODES FOR WIDTH & RAILING REQUIREMENTS

USE A POINT OF RADIUS TO DRAW THE TREADS ON A CURVED STAIRWAY. DRAW CIRCULAR FORMS WITH TEMPLATE OR COMPASS

UP

CHAPTER four

Furniture and Plants Drawn in Plan View

ou must be a successful salesperson to be a winning designer. If you cannot sell your ideas or designs to your client, are you a designer? Adding furniture and plants to your drawings will serve two purposes. First, you will want to verify that you have provided functional layouts with appropriate clearances. Second, you will be able to communicate your ideas to your client. Drawing furniture in your floor plans in a presentation style takes your drawings from very plain to striking.

This chapter, as well as the following chapters, will show you how to draw interior floor plans and elevations as small works of art. Your clients will be impressed by how well you have thought out and presented your ideas.

CHAIRS

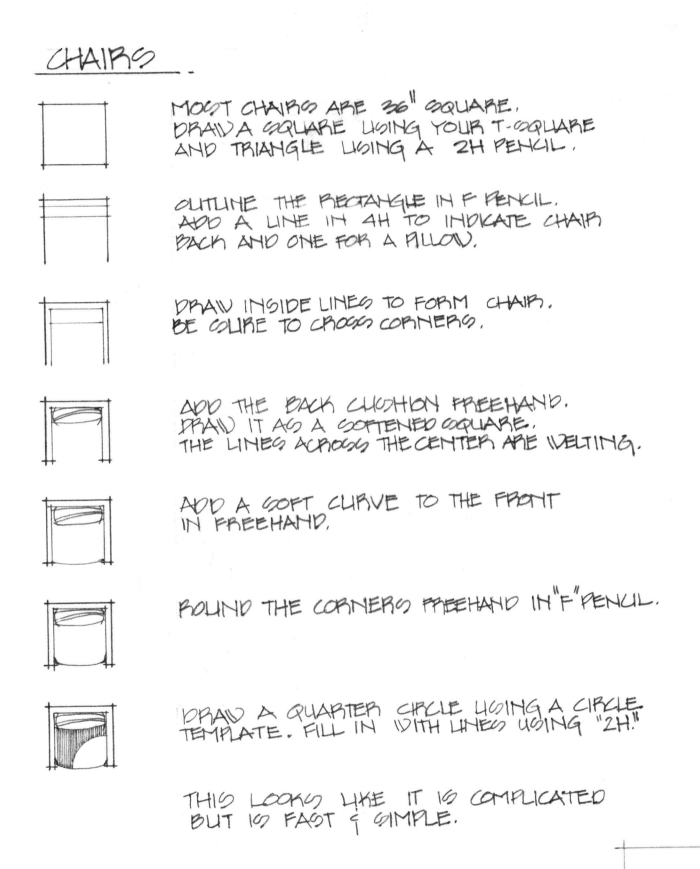

MOST CHAIRS ARE 36" SQUARE.
DRAW A SQUARE USING YOUR T-SQUARE
AND TRIANGLE USING A 2H PENCIL.

OUTLINE THE RECTANGLE IN F PENCIL.
ADD A LINE IN 4H TO INDICATE CHAIR
BACK AND ONE FOR A PILLOW.

DRAW INSIDE LINES TO FORM CHAIR.
BE SURE TO CROSS CORNERS.

ADD THE BACK CUSHION FREEHAND.
DRAW IT AS A SOFTENED SQUARE.
THE LINES ACROSS THE CENTER ARE WELTING.

ADD A SOFT CURVE TO THE FRONT
IN FREEHAND.

ROUND THE CORNERS FREEHAND IN "F" PENCIL.

DRAW A QUARTER CIRCLE USING A CIRCLE
TEMPLATE. FILL IN WITH LINES USING "2H."

THIS LOOKS LIKE IT IS COMPLICATED
BUT IS FAST & SIMPLE.

MORE SQUARE CHAIRS

 SHORTEN THE ARMS OF THE ORIGINAL DESIGN.

 DRAW THE SAME CHAIR ROUNDING THE ENTIRE FRONT.

 OR JUST ROUND THE CENTER OF THE CHAIR.

  CUT IN BACK EITHER TOTALLY WITH DRAFTING EQUIPMENT OR PARTIALLY FREE HAND.

 DRAW CLASSIC EAMES CHAIR PART FREE HAND. YOU CAN DRAW ANY CHAIR SMALLER OR LARGER.

 DRAW A KNOLL BARCELA CHAIR WITH JUST A FEW LINES.

*NOTE:
    CLUB CHAIRS ARE 36"

SMALLER SQUARE CHAIRS

 SMALLER 24" CHAIR IN BLOCK STYLE WORKS FOR DINING ROOM.

 MAKE CHAIRS DISTINCT WITH LITTLE MODIFICATIONS.

 ADD A SHADOW.

 ROUND THE ARMS AND ADD AN OTTOMAN TO MAKE A LOUNGE CHAIR.

 DRAW FREEHAND WITH SHADOWS FOR A DIFFERENT LOOK.

 ADD A BACK FOR AN OFFICE CHAIR.

 OR ADD THE ILLUSION OF A BACK.

 OR MAKE IT LOOK ATTACHED.

✱ NOTE:
OFFICE CHAIRS ARE 18+IN.
DINING ROOM CHAIRS
ARE 22+ INCHES

CLUB CHAIR / OFFICE CHAIR

 CLUB CHAIRS ARE GENERALLY 36" SO START WITH 3/4" CIRCLE IN 1/4" SCALE. DRAW WITH 2H OR 4H.

 DARKEN HALF OF THE CIRCLE WITH 'H' PENCIL.

 EXTEND LINES TO EDGE OF CIRCLE.

 DRAW ACROSS BOTTOM FORMING SHAPE.

 DRAW INTERIOR TO CHAIR USING A SMALLER CIRCLE AND EXTEND TO THE FRONT LINE.

 DRAW ANOTHER CIRCLE TO DRAW SHADOW TO DEFINE THE CHAIR.

  THE SHADOW CAN BE DRAWN A COUPLE OF DIFFERENT WAYS. NOTE THE EMPHASIS AT THE BEGINNING AND END OF EVERY LINE.

CHAIR VARIATION

ROUND THE FRONT OF THE CHAIR
AND DRAW THE SHADOW BY HAND,
THIS GIVES A SOFTER LOOK.

DRAW THE CHAIR SHORTER.

DRAW THE SAME CHAIR WITH
STRAIGHT ARMS.

THE CHAIR CAN BE DRAWN SMALLER
BY USING 1/2" CIRCLE ON THE
CIRCLE TEMPLATE.

YOU CAN ADD ARMS AND
SHADOWS FOR DIVERSITY.

EXTEND THE SIDES AT A 10 DEGREE
ANGLE USING AN ADJUSTABLE
TRIANGLE FOR A DIFFERENT LOOK.

ROUND THE LINES FOR ANOTHER
LOOK AND ADD SHADING.

OR DON'T ADD SHADING.

DRAWING SOFAS

MOST SOFAS ARE 36" DEEP.
DRAW A RECTANGLE USING A "2H" PENCIL.
USE YOUR TRIANGLE AND T-SQUARE.

OUTLINE THE RECTANGLE IN "F" PENCIL.
ADD A LINE IN "4H" PENCIL TO INDICATE
SOFA BACK AND ONE FOR PILLOWS.

DRAW INSIDE LINES IN "4" PENCIL
TO FORM THE BACK OF THE SOFA.
BE SURE TO CROSS CORNERS.

DIVIDE INTO THREE SECTIONS OR
INTO TWO DEPENDING ON
SIZE OR DESIGN.

DRAW THE PILLOWS FREEHAND
USING THE "H" PENCIL.

ROUND THE CORNERS FREEHAND
USING "F" PENCIL.

DRAW AN ARCH USING A CIRCLE
TEMPLATE AND "H" PENCIL.
FINISH HARDLINE VERTICAL LINES.
THE SOFA IS COMPLETE.

SOFA VARIETY

YOUR SIMPLE SOFA CAN BE CHANGED AND SIMPLY BECOME INTERESTING.

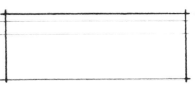

DRAW THE OUTSIDE EDGE IN "F" PENCIL. ADD A LINE IN 4H PENCIL TO INDICATE SOFA BACK AND PILLOW ROW.

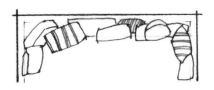

DRAW IN PILLOWS IN "H" PENCIL. HAVE FUN!

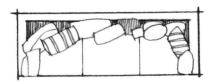

DIVIDE INTO THIRDS OR HALF. DARKEN SPACES BEHIND PILLOWS.

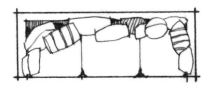

ROUND THE CORNERS FREEHAND IN "F".

LEAVE LIKE THIS OR ADD SHADOW.

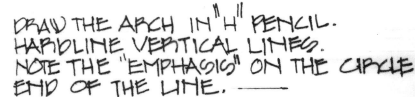

DRAW THE ARCH IN "H" PENCIL. HARDLINE VERTICAL LINES. NOTE THE "EMPHASIS" ON THE CIRCLE END OF THE LINE. ———

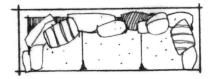

USE DOTS FOR TEXTURE.

* NOTE:
  SOFAS ARE 36" DEEP +

MORE SOFAS

SECTIONAL- DRAW SIMILAR TO SOFAS

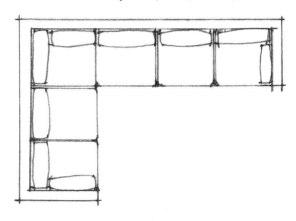

CHAISE

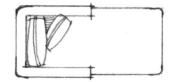

SOFA WITH CHAISE

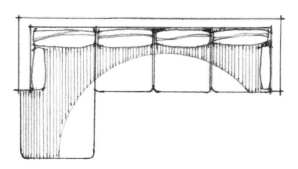

NOTE THE SHADOW ADDS
DEPTH TO THE DRAWING.

AND MORE SOFA STYLES

CIRCULAR SOFAS WORK IF YOU MAKE
THEM SPACIOUS ENOUGH ~~FOR KNEE SPACE~~.

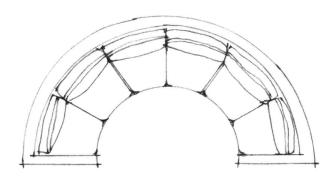

THIS SIZE WORKS.

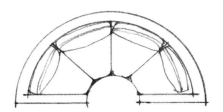

THIS SIZE DOES <u>NOT</u> WORK. IT LOOKS
GOOD ON PAPER, BUT YOUR KNEES DO
NOT FIT IN THE MIDDLE.

HISTORICAL OR VICTORIAN

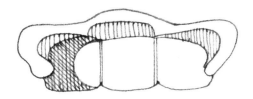

DRAWING TABLES WITH CHAIRS

CHAIRS AROUND A TABLE CAN BE SPACED
USING THE TECHNIQUE SHOWN BELOW.

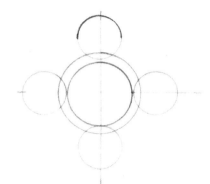

DRAW THE SPACING OF CHAIRS USING CIRCLES.

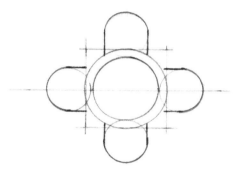

START TO ADD DETAIL.

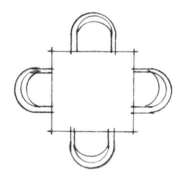

FINISH THE DETAIL ~ DO THIS THEN TRACE.

OTHER TABLES WITH CHAIRS

USE THE SAME TECHNIQUE FOR CHAIRS
THAT ARE NOT PARTLY UNDER THE TABLE.

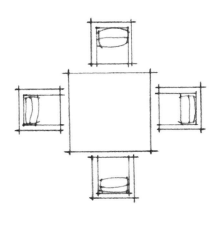

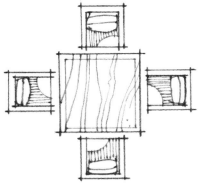

THEN HAVE FUN ADDING DETAIL.

DRAWING BEDS

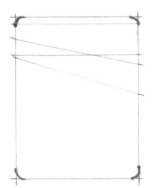

DRAW THE OUTLINE OF THE BED.
DRAW THE CORNERS BY HAND.

DARKEN IN THE OUTSIDE LINE.
NOTICE THE FOLD-DOWN AREA IS
EXTENDED.

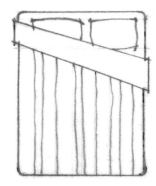

USE THE LINES TO DRAW IN THE
PILLOWS FREEHAND.
ADD DESIGN OF YOUR CHOICE.

BED SIZES

TWIN	39 × 75
FULL	54 × 75
QUEEN	60 × 80
KING	76 × 80
CA KING	72 × 84

BED DESIGN IDEAS

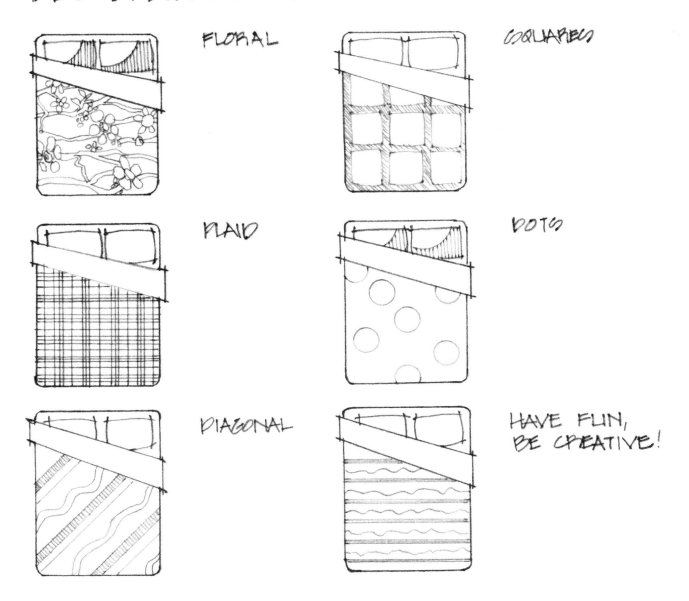

FLORAL

SQUARES

PLAID

DOTS

DIAGONAL

HAVE FUN,
BE CREATIVE!

ADDITIONAL FURNITURE

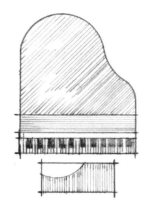

GRAND PIANO

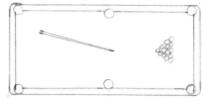

POOL TABLE

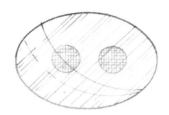

GLASS TOP TABLE

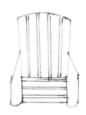

ADIRONDACK CHAIR

Many of the chairs, sofas, and table and chairs will be used for both residential and commercial design.

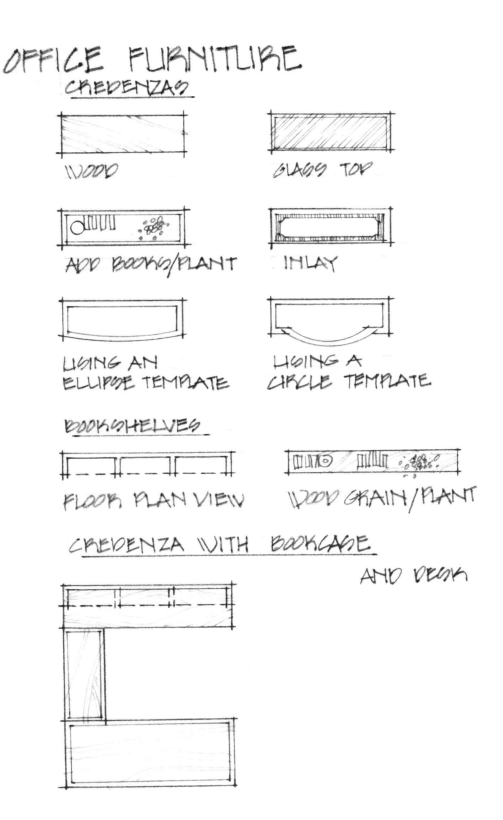

OFFICE FURNITURE

CREDENZAS

WOOD

GLASS TOP

ADD BOOKS/PLANT

INLAY

USING AN ELLIPSE TEMPLATE

USING A CIRCLE TEMPLATE

BOOKSHELVES

FLOOR PLAN VIEW

WOOD GRAIN/PLANT

CREDENZA WITH BOOKCASE

AND DESK

MORE OFFICE FURNITURE

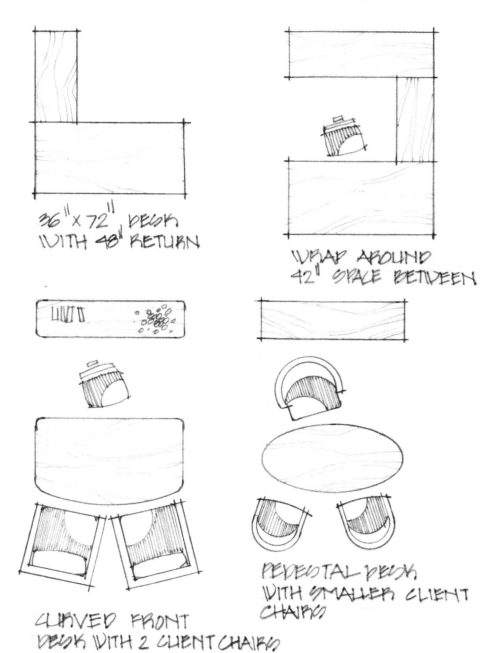

36" x 72" DESK
WITH 48" RETURN

WRAP AROUND
42" SPACE BETWEEN

CURVED FRONT
DESK WITH 2 CLIENT CHAIRS

PEDESTAL DESK
WITH SMALLER CLIENT
CHAIRS

FILING CABINETS

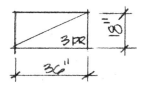
3 DR   8"
36"

3 DR

PLAN VIEW

ALWAYS PROVIDE
ENOUGH CLEAR FLOOR
SPACE IN FRONT OF
CABINETS FOR ACCESS

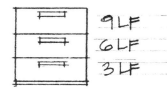
9 LF
6 LF
3 LF

ELEVATION

- SINCE THE CABINET IS 3'-0" WIDE EACH DRAWER HOLDS 3 LINEAR FEET OF FILING. THIS CABINET PROVIDES 9 LINEAR FEET.

- FILE CABINETS GO UP TO 5 DRAWER GENERALLY DESIGNERS PREFER TO USE 2 OR 3 DRAWER AND PLACE A TOP ON IT TO PROVIDE EXTRA WORK SPACE.

RECEPTION DESKS

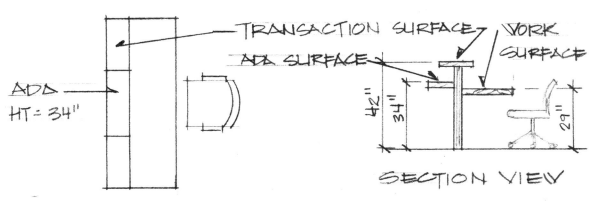

ADA
HT = 34"

TRANSACTION SURFACE   WORK SURFACE

ADA SURFACE

42"   34"   29"

SECTION VIEW

PLAN VIEW

YOU CAN HAVE FUN WITH YOUR RECEPTION DESK DESIGNS BY VARYING SHAPES & MATERIALS

PLANTS IN PLAN VIEW

Adding beautifully drawn plants to a floor plan, elevation, perspective drawing, or sketch can give it a new dimension by giving the impression of depth. Using gray markers as shadow in the plants further defines an area or areas. Plants can make it easier to show size in exterior drawings by comparing tree size to building size. They improve a drawing by grounding a building in a setting or can be used in the foreground to frame a drawing. Examples are shared in this section.

Please note that trees do not look like and should not be drawn as "stick characters." It is easy to add any of the trees suggested in this section and improve the overall appearance of your sketch or rendering. If you have done your drawing in SketchUp, it is easy to trace the drawing and add your personality to the work by hand drawing the trees.

CHAPTER FOUR

PLANTS

PLANTS ADD PERSONALITY TO ANY DRAWING.
START WITH A CIRCLE FOR INDIVIDUAL PLANTS.
CLUSTER PLANTS TOGETHER.

DRAW THE CIRCLE.

 DRAW STRAIGHT LINES WITH TRIANGLE.

 OR DRAW FREEHAND.

 OUTSIDE BORDER LINES FREEHAND
WITH TWO CIRCLES. I LEFT IT PARTLY
UNFINISHED TO SHOW TECHNIQUE.

SQUIGGLE OR FERN STYLE IS SHOWN
IN TWO STEPS. DRAW THE ARMS.
ADD SQUIGGLY LINES TO FORM
PLANTS. SIMPLE & ATTRACTIVE.

SIMPLE & LOOSE. EASY TO DRAW.
JUST DRAWN LOOSELY ON THE PERIMETER.

MORE PLANT DESIGNS

 LEAF-SHAPED PLANT

 SMALL IRREGULAR CIRCLES FORM AN INTERESTING LOOK.

 INDIVIDUAL LEAVES

 CLUSTER PLANTS IN GROUPS. BE SURE TO OVERLAP.

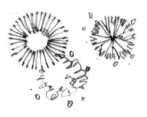 ADD A LITTLE VARIETY TO THE PLANTS IN CLUSTERS.

 OR JUST DRAW TWO PLANTS.

PLANT VARIATIONS

 ALWAYS START WITH A CIRCLE AND ADD DIFFERENT FINISH STYLES.

 QUICKLY DRAW A PERIMETER.

OR

 ADD INTERIOR ELEMENTS.

OR

 COMBINE SEVERAL STYLES.

 DRAW LARGER TO REPRESENT A TREE.

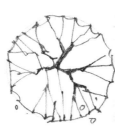 SIMPLIFY THE DRAWING.

MORE PLANT VARIATIONS

 EXTEND THE SIMPLE & LOOSE STYLE TO THE INTERIOR OF THE CIRCLE.

 ADD CIRCLES TO SOFTEN THE EDGES.

 EXTEND THE WIGGLY LINES TO LOOK LIKE BRANCHES.

 ADD A PLANTER BOX.

 OR ADD A POT.

 ADD CIRCLES TO FERN DESIGN.

AND MORE

 ADD CIRCLES TO STRAIGHT LINES.

 ADD CURVED BRANCHES.

 COMBINE CURVED BRANCHES WITH CIRCLES.

 ADD A DEFINED PERIMETER.

 BE CREATIVE.

BE CAREFUL NOT TO MAKE MISTAKES.

TOO LARGE   TOO SMALL   TO SPARSE   LEAVES TOO BIG FOR SCALE

GENERAL NOTES ON FURNITURE LAYOUT

- Furniture is generally dimensioned in inches rather than feet and inches.
- Be sure to refer to graphic standards and manufacturer specifications for sizes and recommended clearances.
- Always provide adequate clearance for the purpose of the space.
  - Corridors
    - 36" minimum—Residential
    - 44" minimum—Commercial (60" is recommended)
  - Circulation space within rooms
    - 30" minimum—Residential
    - 36" minimum—Commercial
- Provide 60" turning radius for ADA clearance at corridor intersections and within necessary rooms.
- Think about the clear floor space in front of cabinets/dressers with door and drawer openings. Imagine a person bending over to get to the bottom drawer once it is open.
- Provide sufficient clearance around furniture.
  - Beds—36" minimum
  - Dining tables—48" minimum
- When placing seating perpendicular, always set one piece back and over so that people seated have enough space for their feet.
- For viewing a television screen, be sure to set the seating area ten feet or more from the screen and consider the size of the screen.
- Use your common sense and walk through the space in your mind to visualize the clearances.
- Be creative with your furniture layouts, but also make sure the space is functional.

EXAMPLE FLOOR PLANS WITH CLEARANCES

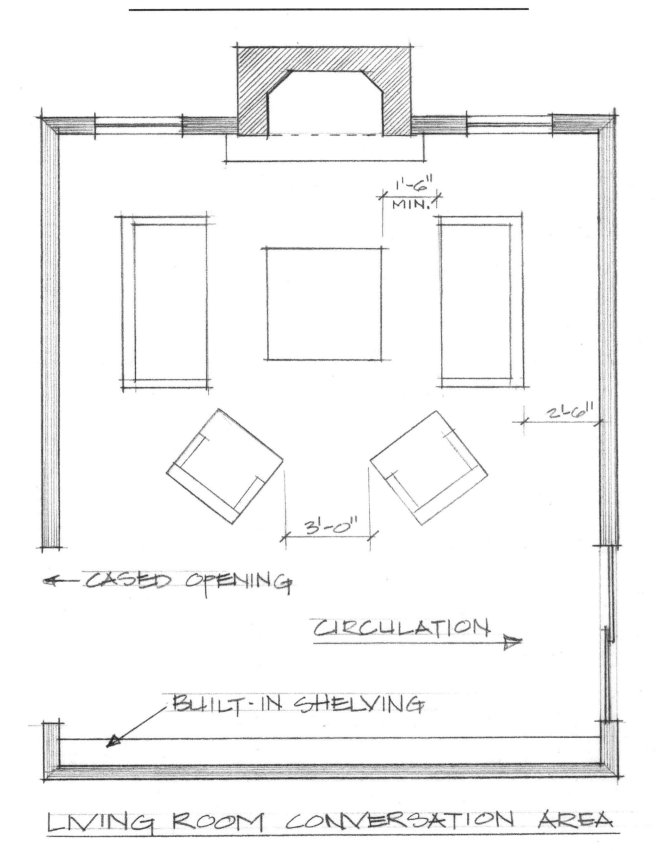

1'-6" MIN.

2'-0"

3'-0"

← CASED OPENING

CIRCULATION →

BUILT-IN SHELVING

LIVING ROOM CONVERSATION AREA

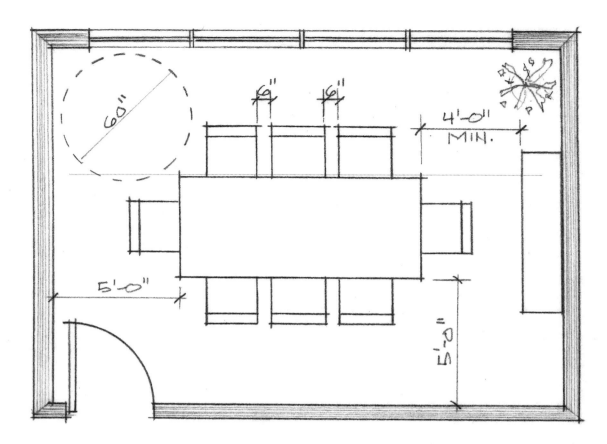

6"   6"

60"

4'-0"
MIN.

5'-0"

5'-0"

DINING OR CONFERENCE ROOM

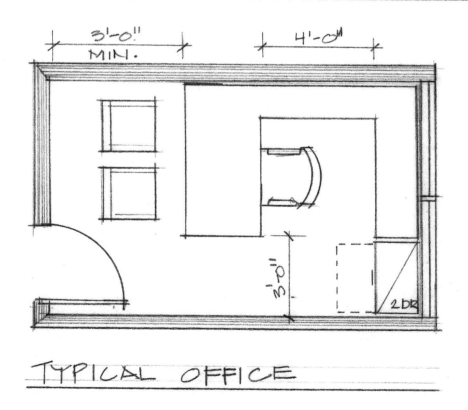

3'-0"
MIN.

4'-0"

3'-0"

2 DR

TYPICAL OFFICE

CHAPTER five

Drawing Interior Materials in Plan View

T his chapter will illustrate how to draw interior flooring as a background using different tile and wood patterns, bamboo, concrete, and marble. When communicating your design intent, it is important to include flooring materials, patterns, and items such as rugs. Flooring in a presentation-style floor plan should be executed using a light hand, so that it does not overwhelm your drawing. Using a 2H or 4H pencil will enable you to illustrate the flooring design and texture without detracting from the overall drawing.

The exception to using a 2H or 4H in flooring is when drawing dots for carpeting. An F pencil should be used when drawing dots to show carpeting texture. One of the important factors in drawing dots to give texture to carpeting, or anything else, is not to draw "tails" on the dots. Examples of good and bad dots are included in this chapter.

When you have designed a unique floor pattern, you will need to communicate this to the installer. A detailed floor plan with the layout is necessary. An example of a detailed flooring pattern is given in this chapter.

TILE FLOORING

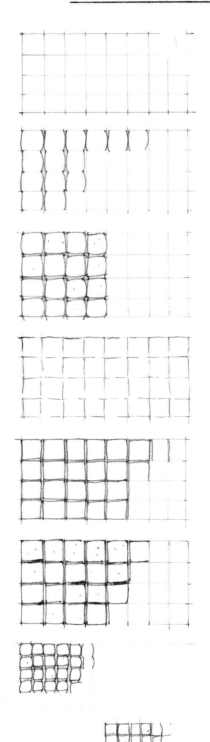

12"x12" CAN BE DRAWN IN MANY WAYS.
DRAW A GRID IN 1/4"SCALE LIGHTLY
WITH A 2H PENCIL.

12"x12" TILES CAN BE ROUNDED FREEHAND.
DRAW THE VERTICAL LINES FIRST
USING A 2H PENCIL.

NEXT DRAW THE HORIZONTAL LINES
USING A 2H PENCIL.
ADD A FEW DOTS TO MAKE IT INTERESTING.
USE AN "F" PENCIL FOR THE DOTS.

12"x12" TILE WITH SOFT LINE
DRAW THE VERTICAL FIRST IN 2H.
THEN DRAW HORIZONTALS.
SOFTLY BREAK THE LINES.

12"x12" TILES CAN BE SQUARED FREEHAND
USING THE SAME TECHNIQUE AS DESCRIBED.
VERTICAL FIRST — THEN HORIZONTAL.
DRAW LINES STRAIGHT AS YOU CAN.

ADD DOTS FOR CHARACTER.
CONNECT SOME SQUARES.

8"x8" TILES CAN BE DRAWN USING THE
SAME TECHNIQUES AS ABOVE
AND DETAILED THE SAME.

MORE TILE FLOORING

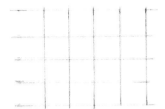

TILE CAN BE DRAWN IN A SIMPLE MANNER AND BE EFFECTIVE. ALWAYS BEGIN WITH A LIGHT GRID DRAWN WITH A 4H PENCIL.

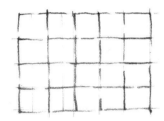

TRACE THE 4H GRID WITH 2H PENCIL WITH VARYING PRESSURE AND BREAKS IN THE LINES.

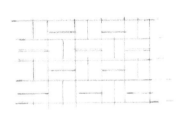

6" x 12" BASKET WEAVE BEGINS WITH A 12" x 12" GRID, DIVIDED AND DRAWN FREEHAND.

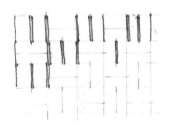

DRAW THE VERTICAL LINES FIRST. PLACE TWO LINES CLOSE TOGETHER TO SHOW GROUT LINES.

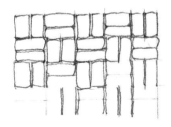

FINISH BY DRAWING THE HORIZONTAL LINES. THIS IS A FREE-HAND STYLE.

ADDITIONAL TILE FLOORING

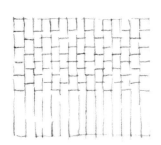 4" x 8" RUNNING BOND IS DRAWN OVER A 4" x 4" GRID FREEHAND.

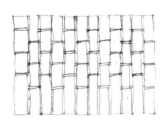 6" x 12" RUNNING BOND IS DRAWN IN A SIMILAR MANNER, ADDING DOUBLE LINES TO SHOW GROUT.

ADD DOTS FOR INTEREST.

 NATURAL STONE FLOORS CAN BE A DYNAMIC ADDITION TO A DESIGN IF DONE CORRECTLY.

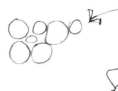 DO NOT DRAW ROCKS LIKE CIRCLES.
DO NOT CONNECT WITH NO SPACE BETWEEN SHAPES.

GRANITE & CONCRETE

GRANITE IS AVAILABLE IN MANY DIFFERENT LOOKS, FROM MEDIUM TO COARSE TEXTURE.
& COARSE GRANITE

MEDIUM TEXTURE GRANITE CAN BE DRAWN IN A SIMPLE MANNER.
& MEDIUM GRANITE

CONCRETE FLOORS TAKE MANY LOOKS. MOST OFTEN THEY ARE DESIGNED WITH EXPANSION JOINTS.

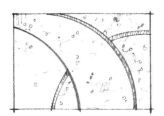

CONCRETE WITH EXPANSION JOINTS CAN BE USED TO FORM PATTERNS.

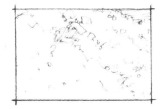

CONCRETE DRAWN AS IN AN OLD LOFT

FLOORING & PAVING

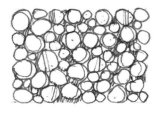

COBBLESTONE IS DRAWN WITH A VARIETY OF CIRCLES. CONNECT WITH SHORT LINES.

RECTANGULAR CUT STONE

RANDOM FLAGSTONE MUST BE DRAWN AT THE RIGHT SCALE.

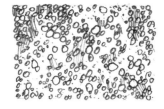

TERRAZZO CAN BE DRAWN AS PEBBLES.

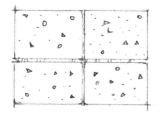

OR TERRAZZO CAN BE DRAWN AS SIMPLY AS SHOWN HERE.

WOOD FLOORING

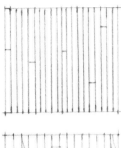

3" WIDE WOOD FLOORING
* DON'T FORGET WOOD COMES IN 8'-0"
   LENGTHS, SO ADD RANDOM END POINTS.

4" WOOD STRIPS WITH A LITTLE GRAIN
MEASURE 1'-0" INCREMENTS FIRST,
THEN DIVIDE INTO THIRDS. ALL IN "H" PENCIL,
ADD RANDOM END POINTS & GRAIN.
GRAIN IS MORE STRAIGHT THAN CURVY.

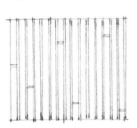

4" WOOD STRIPS WITH A DOUBLE LINE
DRAW SAME AS 4" WOOD ABOVE WITH ONE
MORE LINE AND NO WOOD GRAIN.

4" WOOD STRIPS WITH A DOUBLE LINE
   AND SOME WOOD GRAIN
USE "H" PENCIL UNLESS YOU HAVE WHAT
I CALL A "HEAVY" HAND, THEN USE "2H" PENCIL.

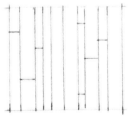

RANDOM WIDTHS AND LENGTHS
SIMPLE AND EASY!
USE WHEN YOU DON'T HAVE MUCH TIME.

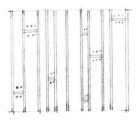

ADD DOUBLE LINES AND PEGS.
FUN AND A LITTLE MORE RUSTIC.

OLD WORLD WOOD FLOORING

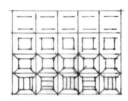

PARQUET WOOD ORNATE
   DRAW HORIZONTAL LINES FIRST,
   ADD THE VERTICAL LINES,
   MITER THE CORNERS,
   ADD THE LAST DETAIL - THE STRIPES.

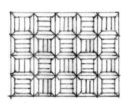

FINISHED ORNATE WOOD FLOORING
TIME CONSUMING, BUT BEAUTIFUL!

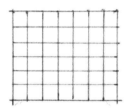

8" WOOD PARQUET IS SIMPLER,
USE YOUR STRAIGHT EDGE AND TRIANGLE
TO DRAW SQUARES.

DRAW THE INSIDE LINES (WOOD STRIPS)
FREE HAND WITH "2H" PENCIL.
HERE YOU HAVE SIMPLE WOOD PARQUET.

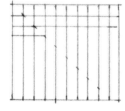

6" WOOD PARQUET IS DONE IN SAME TECHNIQUE.
IF YOU DRAW A 45° LINE ACROSS THE LINES
YOUR 6" INCREMENTS WILL EASILY BE MARKED
AND ACCURATELY.

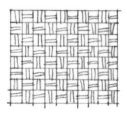

6" WOOD PARQUET IS SIMPLE AND ELEGANT.

MORE WOOD FLOORING

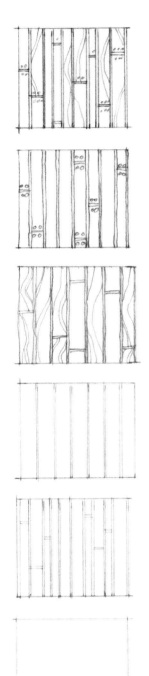

RANDOM WIDTHS AND LENGTHS
ADD WOOD GRAIN IN "2H" PENCIL.
KEEP IT SIMPLE - NOT TOO CURVY.

RANDOM WIDTHS CAN BE DRAWN FREEHAND.
START BY DRAFTING IN "2H" PENCIL
THEN DRAW FREEHAND IN "H" PENCIL.

8" BOARDS CAN BE DRAWN FREEHAND
SAME AS STYLE ABOVE.
ADD IN SIMPLE WOOD GRAIN IN "2H" PENCIL.

NOW...
    YOU FILL IN THE FREEHAND LINES.
    8" BOARDS

FREEHAND OVER THIS TO PRACTICE
RANDOM WIDTHS AND LENGTHS.

PRACTICE WOOD FLOORING OF YOUR CHOICE.
HAVE FUN!

FUN WOOD FLOORING

8" WOOD PARQUET
CAN BE DRAWN FREEFORM TO SHOW GRAIN.
NOTE ALL GRAIN LINES TOUCH BOTH SIDES.
"2H" PENCIL WORKS BEST.

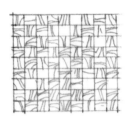

6" WOOD PARQUET
DRAWN EXACTLY AS 8" ONLY SMALLER

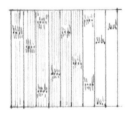

BAMBOO IN 6" STRIPS STARTS WITH DOTS
TO SHOW EDGES.   A FEW SHORT STROKES
EXTEND FROM THE DOTS
THIN LINES IN "4H" PENCIL FORM THE GRAIN.

RECYCLED WOOD IS USUALLY RANDOM PLANKING,
KNOTS AND SCRATCH MARKS AND HOLES ARE
COMMON.
USE YOUR IMAGINATION OR COPY MINE.
"2H" PENCIL WORKS BEST.

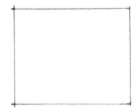

YOUR TURN...
DRAW THE FLOOR OF YOUR CHOICE.

CARPETING

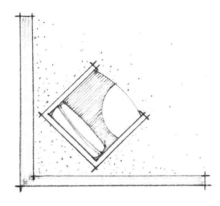

CARPET IS SHOWN BY A SERIES OF DOTS DRAWN WITH AN "F" PENCIL WITH MORE DOTS CLOSE TO THE WALLS AND FURNITURE.

DO NOT DRAW TAILS WITH YOUR DOTS.

DOTS WITH TAILS LOOK <u>BAD</u>.

← DON'T DO CARPET LIKE THIS.

DEFINE STAIRS WITH DOTS TO SHOW DEPTH.

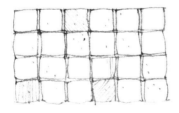

THE SAME DOTS CAN BE ADDED TO TILE TO CHANGE THE LOOK.

AREA RUGS

AREA RUGS ADD YOUR PERSONAL STYLE TO A FLOOR PLAN. THE SOURCES FOR AREA RUG DESIGN IDEAS ARE INFINITE. THE INTERNET IS A WONDERFUL SOURCE FOR INSPIRATION. THERE ARE SOME SIMPLE GUIDELINES FOR SUCCESSFUL FULL-LOOKING RUGS

PICK A STANDARD SIZE THAT FITS THE ROOM.

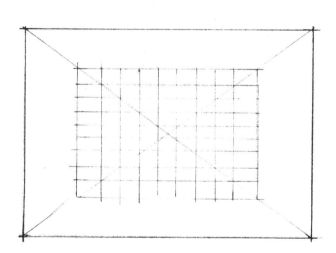

9'-0" x 12'-0"
SKETCH YOUR DESIGN WITH GUIDELINES.

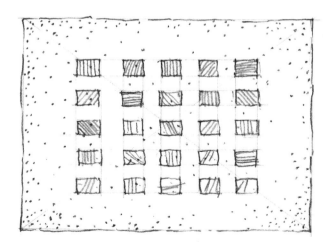

TRACE OVER WITH FREEHAND USING VARIABLE PRESSURE & BROKEN LINE WEIGHT. FILL IN TO MAKE MORE APPEALING DOT LIKE CARPET.

AREA RUG IDEAS

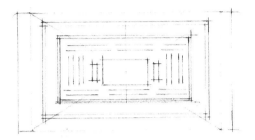

LAYOUT A DETAILED RUG,
ADD A FRINGE ON THE
ENDS FOR INTEREST.

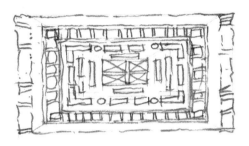

ADD DETAIL WITH
FREEHAND.
ADD FRINGE DETAIL.

CAREFULLY RENDER
ALL DETAILED AREAS.
ADD DOTS.

SIMPLER AREA RUGS

SIMPLE DESIGNS CAN
MAKE A BIG IMPACT.

SOME FUN AREA RUGS

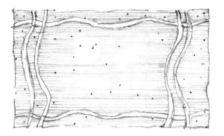

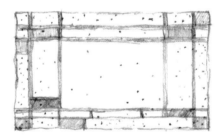
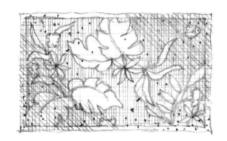

FLOORING DETAIL - FOYER

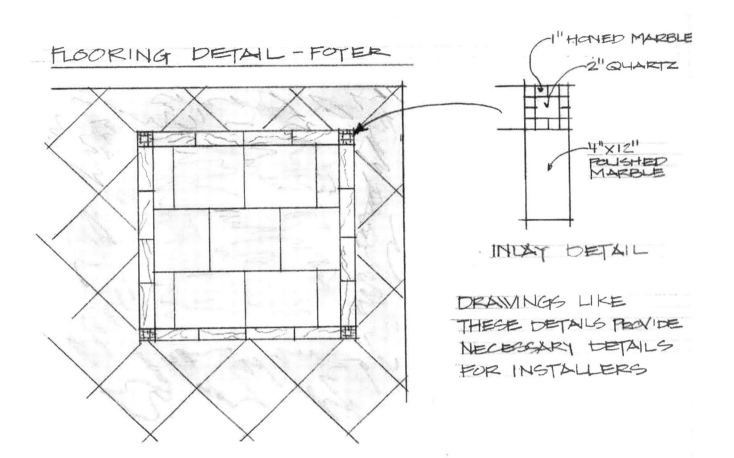

1" HONED MARBLE

2" QUARTZ

4"X12" POLISHED MARBLE

INLAY DETAIL

DRAWINGS LIKE
THESE DETAILS PROVIDE
NECESSARY DETAILS
FOR INSTALLERS

EXAMPLE PLAN WITH FLOORING

1/4"=1'-0"

CHAPTER SIX

Interior Elevations

 single interior can have a million different looks. Designers draw elevations to explore design ideas in the ideation phase of design. Elevations allow you to work out the details and check your balance, proportion, and use of space. Elevations are an easy way to show your client exactly how you see the interior, wall by wall. Your design ideas become very clear with good elevations.

Your elevations can show how the window coverings are to be designed, or how the fireplace is to look, or even what style the cabinets should be. In addition, elevations show placement of windows and doors, art, and mirrors. Elevations allow you to show your client many effects in a more detailed manner. Anything that is placed in the interior can be shown in elevations.

Your elevations can be drawn in ½-inch scale and then copied in a smaller size. This makes the details that you have drawn look much more precise.

This chapter begins by showing how to draw your elevations.

DRAWING ELEVATIONS

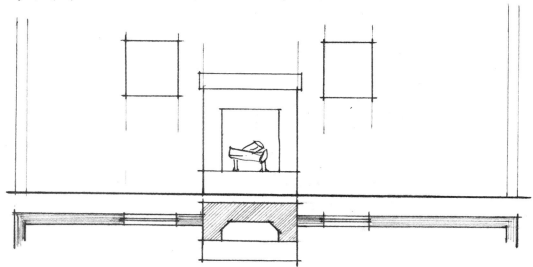

THE ELEVATIONS ARE LAID OUT BY DRAWING LINES
EXTENDING FROM WALL YOU PLAN TO DRAW.
DRAW THE LINES AS IF YOU WERE STANDING IN
FRONT OF THE WALL LOOKING AT IT.

LAY OUT THE WALL ELEVATION IN ¼" SCALE FIRST
TO SEE IF THE PROPORTIONS WORK WELL, THEN
REDRAW IN ½" SCALE TO SHOW MORE DETAIL!

MY ILLUSTRATIONS ARE ALL IN ¼" SCALE
AND ARE TO GIVE YOU IDEAS ONLY.

FURNITURE IN ELEVATION

FURNITURE IN THE ELEVATION IS SIMPLIFIED WITH ENOUGH DETAIL TO KEEP IT INTERESTING, BUT THE BACKGROUND IS WHERE THE EMPHASIS OF THE DRAWING NEEDS TO BE TO SHOW ARCHITECTURAL DETAILS.

DRAWING ITEMS SITTING AT AN ANGLE IN A ROOM

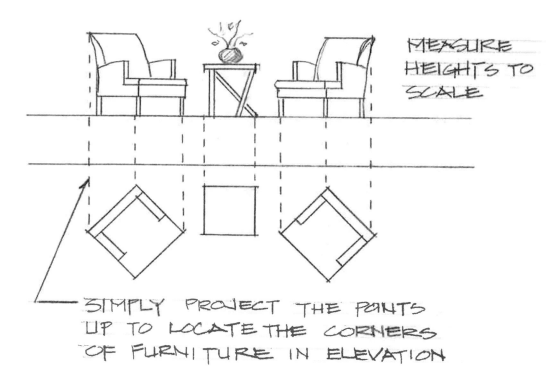

MEASURE HEIGHTS TO SCALE

SIMPLY PROJECT THE POINTS UP TO LOCATE THE CORNERS OF FURNITURE IN ELEVATION

DRAWING WINDOWS

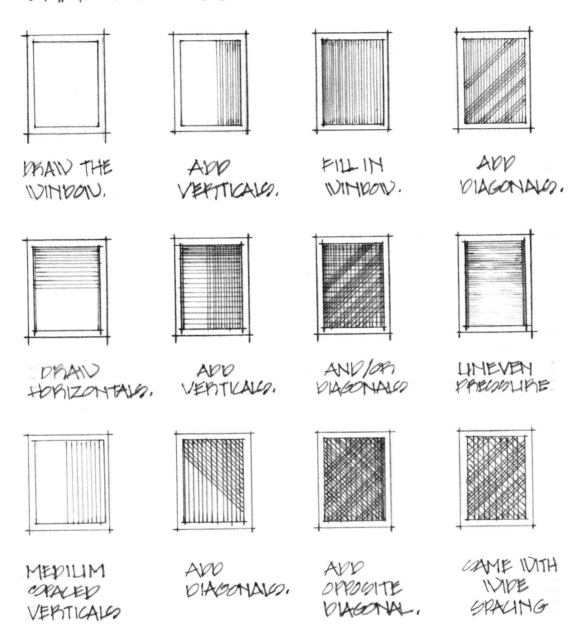

DRAW THE WINDOW.

ADD VERTICALS.

FILL IN WINDOW.

ADD DIAGONALS.

DRAW HORIZONTALS.

ADD VERTICALS.

AND/OR DIAGONALS

UNEVEN PRESSURE

MEDIUM SPACED VERTICALS

ADD DIAGONALS.

ADD OPPOSITE DIAGONAL.

SAME WITH WIDE SPACING

WINDOWS

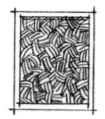

HATCH
TECHNIQUE

2H HATCH
H SHADOW

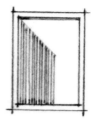

H SHADOW
LINED

FREEHAND
CROSSHATCH

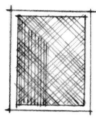

DIAGONALS
WITH SHADOW

MULLIONS
FREEHAND

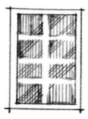

MULLIONS
DIAGONAL

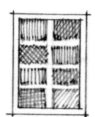

VARIETY

DRAPERIES OUTSIDE VIEW

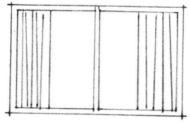 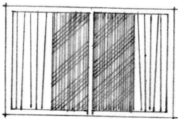 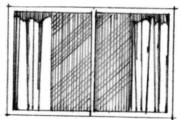

MORE WINDOWS LOOKING OUT

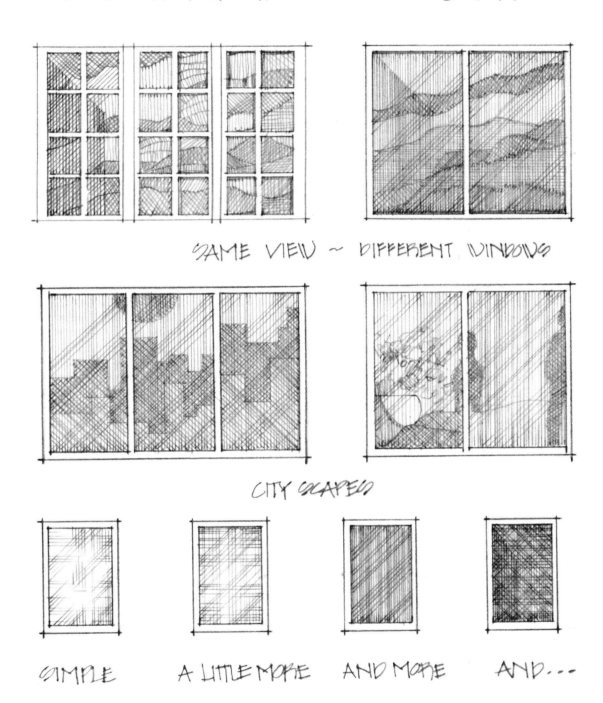

SAME VIEW ~ DIFFERENT WINDOWS

CITY SCAPES

SIMPLE   A LITTLE MORE   AND MORE   AND...

WINDOW COVERINGS

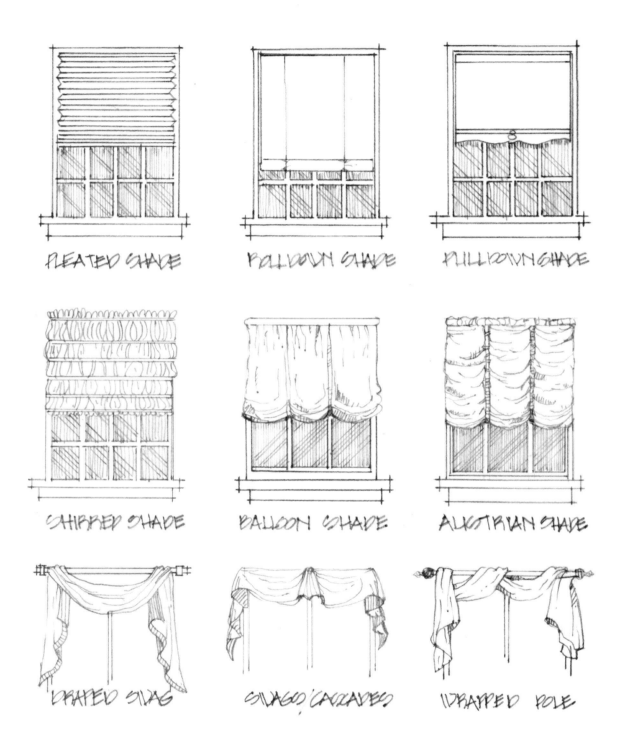

PLEATED SHADE

ROLLDOWN SHADE

PULLDOWN SHADE

SHIRRED SHADE

BALLOON SHADE

AUSTRIAN SHADE

DRAPED SWAG

SWAGS/CASCADES

WRAPPED POLE

DRAPERIES

GEORGIAN TIEBACK

FRENCH PLEAT

CORNICE/HOLDBACK

OVER DRAPERY
VALANCE

WOOD CORNICE
SWAGS/CASCADES

ASYMMETRIC TIE-
BACK/CORNICE BOX

ONE WALL, DIFFERENT STYLES

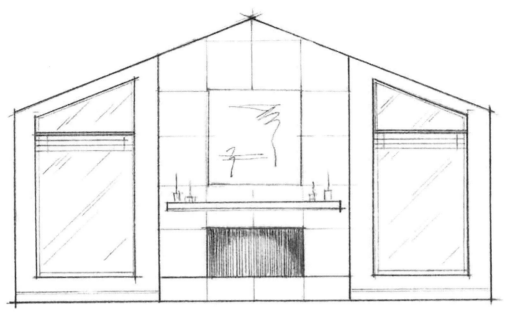

ELEVATION OF ROOM WITH VAULTED CLG.

ELEVATION WITH SLOPED CEILING

LINE WEIGHT IN ELEVATION

HOTE HOW THE LINES GET
LIGHTER AS THEY GO BACK

THIS IS TRUE IN ALL DRAWINGS

CHAPTER Seven

Section Drawings

Sections cut right through a building, an orthographic projection as if cut down the middle by a knife. A section opens the space to show the relevant architectural and structural information. In interior design, the section is used to show the relationships of rooms. Everything can more easily be shown in elevations; however, interior designers use sections to show transition between spaces. Interior designers also use section drawings to show custom detailing for cabinetry, ceiling and soffit detailing, and custom millwork. Sections also allow us to study several floors in a building when it is imperative to understand stairways, window alignment, and the use of spaces in a structure. When designing or redesigning an interior space, designers need to always be aware of what is above and below the space. Sections are a great way to think it through on paper and not make a mistake on a design. For instance, you would not want a cinema room with surround sound below a nursery or even a master bedroom.

Sections and elevations are both vertical drawings; they retain the true proportions, actual scale, and same shape, but elevations show one wall of one room at a time. The relationships between the floors, walls, and roof are shown in section drawings. Door locations and window locations, as well as heights, cabinetry, and stair locations, are also shown.

If you were to draw an architectural section, you would want to show the following:

- Type of foundation
- Floor system
- Wall construction, interior and exterior
- Beam or column sizes and materials
- Wall heights
- Elevation of floors
- Floor members
- Floor sheathing
- Ceiling members
- Roof pitch
- Roof sheathing
- Insulation
- Roof finish material

It is always good to add a human figure to the drawing to help illustrate the scale of the spaces.

The section generally is drawn in ¼- or ⅛-inch scale by interior designers to show how the rooms relate to one another. This chapter includes illustrations of simple sections. Detail sections can be drawn in 1-inch, 1½-inch, or 3-inch scale depending on the amount of material detail necessary. In this chapter you will see examples of a complete structure section, a cabinet section, and sections showing a flooring and a ceiling detail. As interior designers we use these section drawings to communicate our design details to our clients and contractors.

BUILDING SECTION

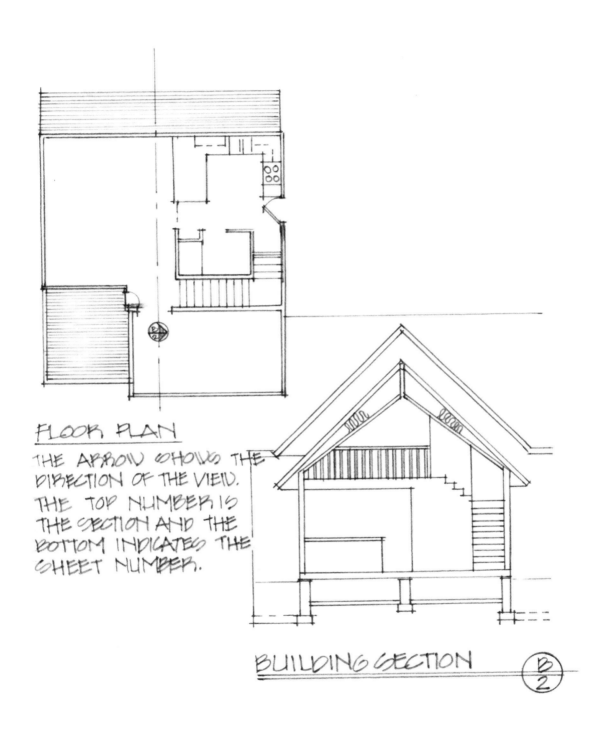

FLOOR PLAN

THE ARROW SHOWS THE DIRECTION OF THE VIEW. THE TOP NUMBER IS THE SECTION AND THE BOTTOM INDICATES THE SHEET NUMBER.

BUILDING SECTION

DEFINITION BY LINE WEIGHT

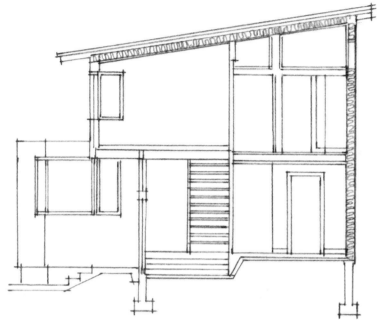

NOTE HOW THE USE OF LINE WEIGHTS ENHANCES THE SENSE OF DEPTH.

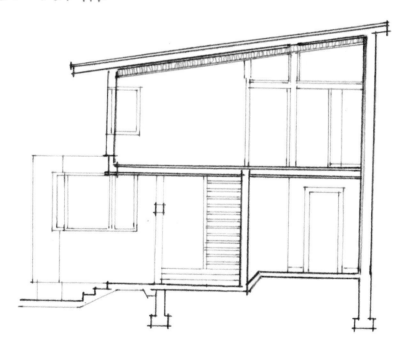

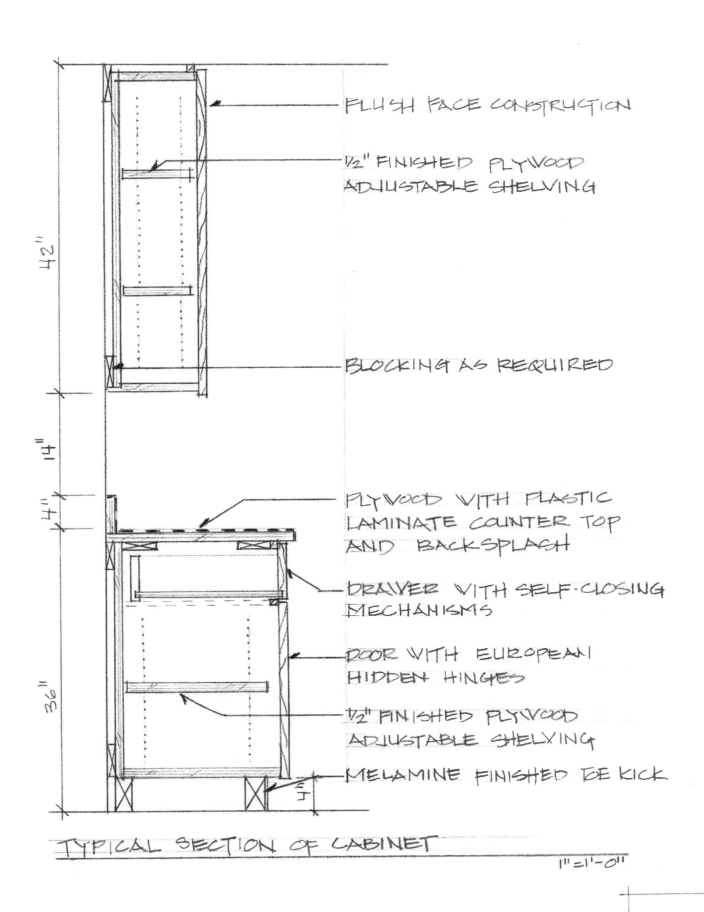

FLUSH FACE CONSTRUCTION

1/2" FINISHED PLYWOOD
ADJUSTABLE SHELVING

BLOCKING AS REQUIRED

PLYWOOD WITH PLASTIC
LAMINATE COUNTER TOP
AND BACKSPLASH

DRAWER WITH SELF-CLOSING
MECHANISMS

DOOR WITH EUROPEAN
HIDDEN HINGES

1/2" FINISHED PLYWOOD
ADJUSTABLE SHELVING

MELAMINE FINISHED TOE KICK

42"

14"

4"

36"

4"

TYPICAL SECTION OF CABINET

1"=1'-0"

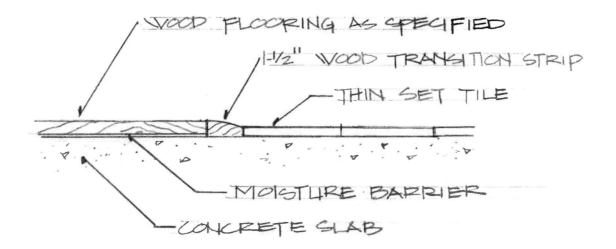

WOOD FLOORING AS SPECIFIED

1-1/2" WOOD TRANSITION STRIP

THIN SET TILE

MOISTURE BARRIER

CONCRETE SLAB

SECTION OF FLOORING TRANSITION

3"=1'-0"

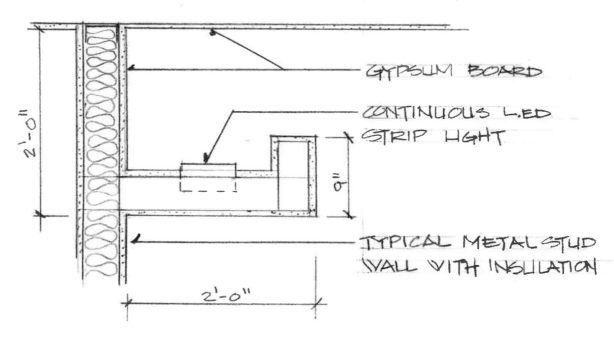

CEILING JOIST

GYPSUM BOARD

CONTINUOUS L.ED STRIP LIGHT

2'-0"

9"

TYPICAL METAL STUD WALL WITH INSULATION

2'-0"

SECTION OF CEILING SOFFIT DETAIL

1"=1'-0"

CHAPTER eight

Electrical and Lighting Plans

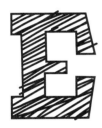lectrical and lighting plans are used to show the locations for electrical outlets, switches, phone lines, and locations for lighting fixtures. For simple residential plans, both electrical and lighting may be shown on one plan. This would be called a lighting/electrical plan. A more complex lighting plan will be labeled as a reflected ceiling plan (RCP). To create an RCP, imagine that you placed a mirror on the floor, and draw all the elements you see on the ceiling. An RCP includes the placement of all fixtures on the ceiling and also HVAC supply and return vents. Most designers will also include wall sconces and under-cabinet lighting on the RCP even though they are not physically on the ceiling. This allows most lighting elements to be shown on the RCP.

RCPs include the following:

- Ceiling materials such as gypsum board or dropped acoustical ceiling
- Ceiling heights
- Location of all lighting fixtures (represented by symbols)
- Switches and electrical loops
- All other elements placed on the ceiling (HVAC, sprinklers, emergency lighting, etc.)

A lighting plan is slightly different from an RCP and includes the following:

- Location of lighting fixtures (represented by symbols)
- Switches and electrical loops
- Location of furniture and cabinetry (they can be drawn with a 2H so that they are a lighter line weight than the symbols)
- Electrical symbols (if the plan is not too complex)

An electrical plan shows the following:

- Locations and types of all electrical outlets
- Locations of all switches, thermostats, etc.

This chapter will give examples of reflected ceiling and electrical plans and the symbols used to represent different types of fixtures, switches, and elements commonly found on these plans.

SWITCH SYMBOLS

SWITCH	NOTES
S	SINGLE SWITCH - TURNS ON ONE OR MORE LIGHTS FROM ONE LOCATION
S₃	3-WAY SWITCH - TURNS ON ONE OR MORE LIGHTS FROM TWO LOCATIONS. NEEDED FOR ROOMS WITH TWO ENTRIES
S₄	4-WAY SWITCH - IS USED TO TURN ON TWO 3-WAY SWITCHES WITH ONE OR MORE LIGHTS FROM THREE LOCATIONS
SSS	ONE LOCATION FOR THREE SWITCHES IN ONE GANG BOX
Sᴅᴍ	DIMMER SWITCH - USED TO CONTROL THE INTENSITY OF THE LIGHT
S₃ᴅᴍ	THREE WAY DIMMER SWITCH - USED TO CONTROL LIGHT INTENSITY FROM TWO LOCATIONS
(stacked SSS)	THREE SWITCHES STACKED AT ONE LOCATION OFTEN USED FOR BATHROOM VENTILATION
Sᴅ	DOOR SWITCH - TURNS ON LIGHT WHEN DOOR IS OPENED PANTRY OR CLOSET USE
(S)	CEILING PULL SWITCH - USED IN ATTICS OR CLOSETS
T	THERMOSTAT - WALL-MOUNTED HEAT CONTROL

RECEPTACLE SYMBOLS

- HEIGHT - HEIGHT ABOVE FLOOR IF NOT STANDARD
- TYPE = TYPE OF RECEPTACLE
SINGLE RECEPTACLE - DEDICATED CIRCUIT

DOUBLE RECEPTACLE - STANDARD DUPLEX GROUNDED RECEPTACLE

QUADRUPLEX RECEPTACLE - TWO GANG BOX WITH FOUR RECEPTACLES

TRIPLEX RECEPTACLE - TWO GANG BOX WITH THREE RECEPTACLES

RECEPTACLE SYMBOLS CONTINUED

DUPLEX RECEPTACLE WITH SWITCH - TWO GANG BOX WITH A DUPLEX RECEPTACLE & A SWITCH

CLOCK RECEPTACLE - AREA IN CENTER IS RECESSED SO A CLOCK FIT FLUSH TO THE WALL

SPLIT-WIRED DUPLEX RECEPTACLE - TOP CONTROLLED BY A SWITCH. USED FOR LAMPS

WATERPROOF RECEPTACLE - COVERED

SINGLE FLOOR RECEPTACLE

DUPLEX FLOOR RECEPTACLE

GROUND FAULT INTERRUPTER - RECEPTACLE PROTECTED BY A GROUND FAULT CIRCUIT INTERRUPTER

RANGE RECEPTACLE - 50 AMP - 4 WIRE

CLOTHES DRYER RECEPTACLE - 30 AMP - 4 WIRE

SINGLE RECEPTACLE WITH SWITCH

FLOOR JUNCTION BOX - CIRCUITS CONNECT IN BOX

BLANKED OUTLET - OUTLET NOT IN USE

JUNCTION BOX - CIRCUITS CONNECT IN BOX

LIGHTING SYMBOLS

CEILING-MOUNTED LIGHT - LABEL WITH TYPE

    FL   FLUORESCENT LAMP

    IN   INCANDESCENT LAMP

    HA   HALOGEN LAMP

EXAMPLE:

WALL-MOUNT FIXTURE

CEILING-MOUNTED WALL-WASHER FIXTURE

LIGHTING SYMBOLS CONTINUED

RECESSED FIXTURE

RECESSED FIXTURE ALTERNATIVE

HANGING CEILING FIXTURE

CEILING-MOUNTED SPOTLIGHT

CEILING-MOUNTED LIGHT TRACK

RECESSED FIXTURE - DAMP LOCATION - USED IN SHOWERS

FLUORESCENT CEILING-MOUNTED FIXTURE

FLUORESCENT LIGHT STRIP

SURFACE-MOUNTED FLUORESCENT

TRACK LIGHTING

TELEPHONE

DATA COMMUNICATIONS OUTLET

TELEVISION OUTLET FOR CABLE

DOOR BELL CHIME

FAN HANGER OUTLET

SMOKE DETECTOR - CEILING MOUNT

WATER HEATER

RADIANT HEAT - CEILING MOUNT

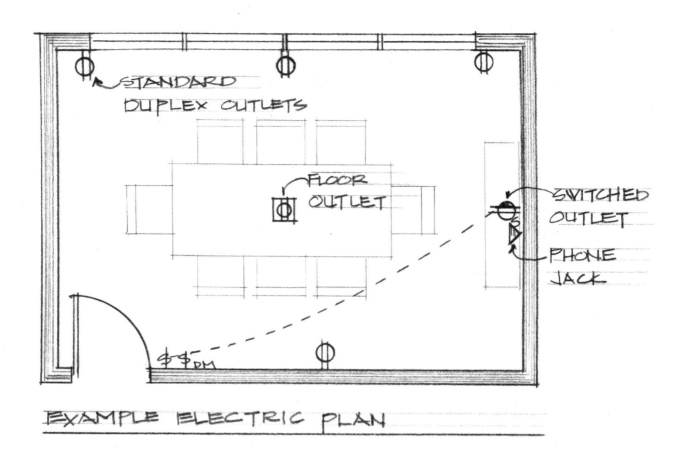

STANDARD
DUPLEX OUTLETS

FLOOR
OUTLET

SWITCHED
OUTLET

PHONE
JACK

$ $DM

EXAMPLE ELECTRIC PLAN

■ OFTEN TIMES SIMPLE ELECTRIC PLANS
  ARE COMBINED WITH A SIMPLE LIGHTING
  PLAN. OR FURNITURE PLAN
■ OUTLETS ARE NOT SHOWN ON RCP's
  UNLESS THEY ARE MOUNTED ON THE CEILING

LEGEND	
⊖	STANDARD DUPLEX OUTLET
⊖	SPLIT SWITCHED OUTLET
⊞	FLOOR OUTLET
◁	PHONE JACK
$	SINGLE POLE SWITCH
$DM	SWITCH W/ DIMMER

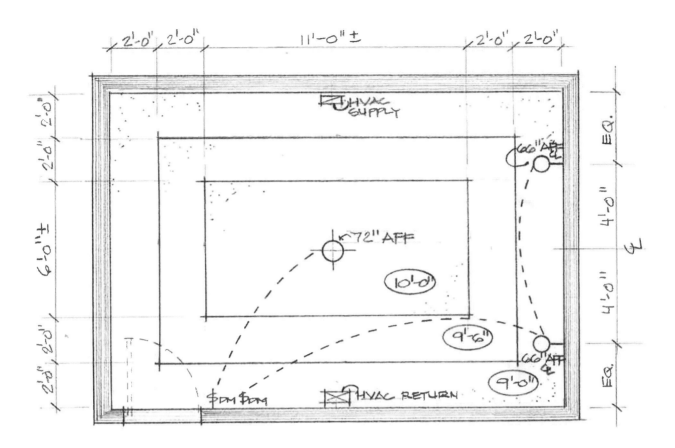

EXAMPLE REFLECTED CEILING PLAN

- ☑ NOTICE THE DOOR IS DASHED, THIS IS BECAUSE IN AN R.C.P. YOU ARE LOOKING AT THE CEILING LEVEL AND MOST DOORS DO NOT GO TO THE CLG.
- ☑ CEILING HEIGHTS ARE NOTED IN THE OVAL SYMBOL. HEIGHTS ARE ALWAYS GIVEN ABOVE FINISHED FLOOR (AFF)
- ☑ WITH GYPSUM BOARD CEILINGS YOU MUST DIMENSION THE LOCATION OF TRAYS, SOFFITS, FIXTURES, ETC.
- ☑ ALL SUSPENDED OR WALL MOUNTED FIXTURES MUST HAVE MOUNTING HEIGHT NOTED.
- ☑ AN RCP SHOWS ALL ELEMENTS ON CEILING INCLUDING HVAC, SPRINKLERS, ETC.
- ☑ USE A FRENCH CURVE TO DRAW THE SWITCHING LOOPS FOR NEATNESS.

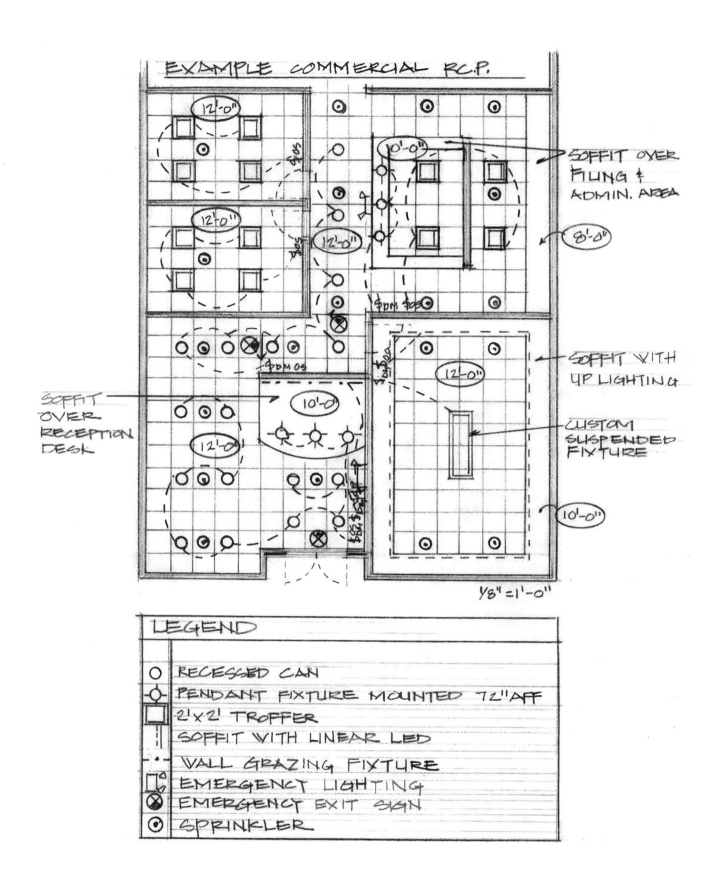

EXAMPLE COMMERCIAL R.C.P.

SOFFIT OVER FILING & ADMIN. AREA

SOFFIT WITH UP LIGHTING

CUSTOM SUSPENDED FIXTURE

SOFFIT OVER RECEPTION DESK

1/8" = 1'-0"

	LEGEND
○	RECESSED CAN
-Ⓧ-	PENDANT FIXTURE MOUNTED 72" AFF
☐	2' x 2' TROFFER
┊	SOFFIT WITH LINEAR LED
·—	WALL GRAZING FIXTURE
☐	EMERGENCY LIGHTING
⊗	EMERGENCY EXIT SIGN
⊙	SPRINKLER

CHAPTER nine

Kitchens and Baths

itchens and bathrooms come in every size and design imaginable. The National Kitchen and Bath Association (NKBA) offers Kitchen Planning and Access Guidelines as well as Bathroom Planning and Access Guidelines online, at www.nkba.org. These comprehensive guides will tell you almost everything you need to know about the basics of layout and design in order to design your kitchen and bath. This chapter will show the basics of drafting kitchen and bath layouts and how to draw the diverse types of fixtures and equipment. Examples of both residential and commercial bathrooms are included.

KITCHENS

There are many books available on kitchen design and layout; the kitchen is the hub of our home. My intention in this chapter is to show the basic layouts used in kitchens over the last few years. I will illustrate the different layouts and elevations used in presentation drawings.

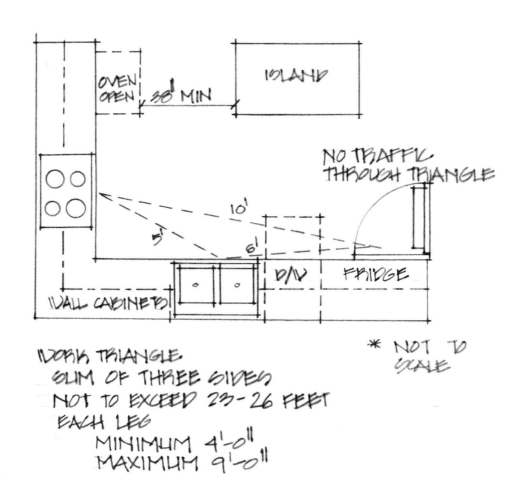

THE L-SHAPED KITCHEN

OVEN OPEN   38' MIN   ISLAND

NO TRAFFIC THROUGH TRIANGLE

10'

5'

6'

D/W   FRIDGE

WALL CABINETS

* NOT TO SCALE

WORK TRIANGLE
SUM OF THREE SIDES
NOT TO EXCEED 23-26 FEET
EACH LEG
MINIMUM 4'-0"
MAXIMUM 9'-0"

CORRIDOR KITCHENS

TWO-PERSON CORRIDOR

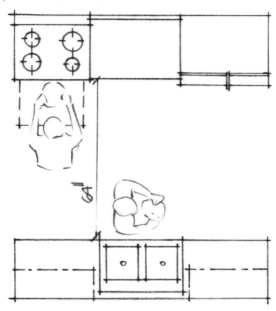

ONE-PERSON CORRIDOR

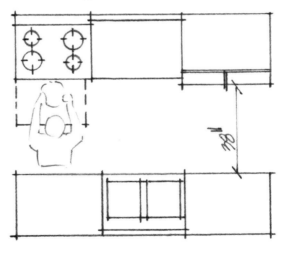

U-SHAPED KITCHEN

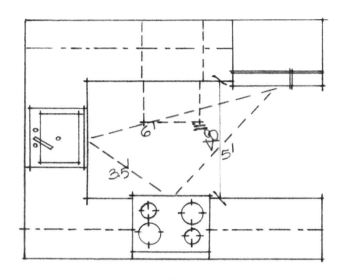

ONE-WALL KITCHEN

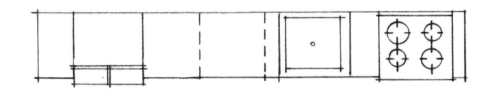

HEIGHT REQUIREMENTS

SPACE REQUIREMENTS

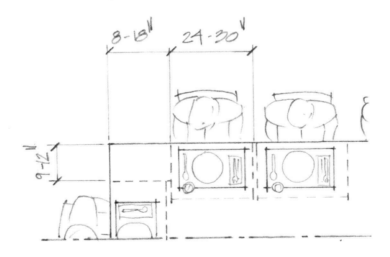

STANDARD SIZES

ITEM	WIDTH/LENGTH	HEIGHT	DEPTH	SPECIAL
KITCHEN COUNTER		36"	24-30"	28" WHEEL CHAIR
REFRIGERATOR	28-60"	5-6'	2'6"	
DISH WASHER	24"	34"	24"	
RANGE	30-36"	36"	24"	
OVEN	24-30"	24-30"	26"	
WASHER	30"	36"	30"	
DRYER	30"	36"	30"	
BATHROOM COUNTER	AS NEEDED	30-36"	24"	
TOILET	15"	28-30"	26"	
BATHTUB	5-7'-8"	16-24"	2'-4"	
INTERIOR DOOR	2'6" - 3'0"	6'8"	1⅜"	
EXTERIOR DOOR	3'-0"	6'-8"	1¾"	
CEILING		8'-0"	8'-0"	

STANDARD HEIGHTS - CABINETS

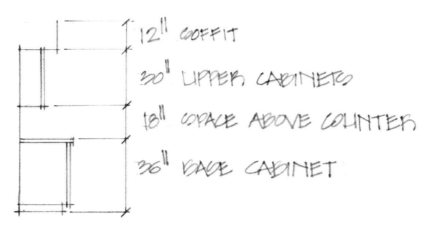

12" SOFFIT

30" UPPER CABINETS

18" SPACE ABOVE COUNTER

36" BASE CABINET

CUSTOM KITCHENS VARY WITH DESIGN, BUT THE BASICS REMAIN THE SAME. NOTE THE FOLLOWING
* 22" OPEN SPACE ABOVE THE SINK
  30" OPEN SPACE ABOVE THE RANGE TOP

PLANNING FOR A BARRIER FREE KITCHEN

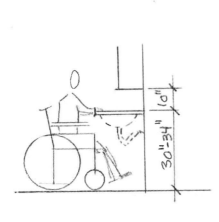
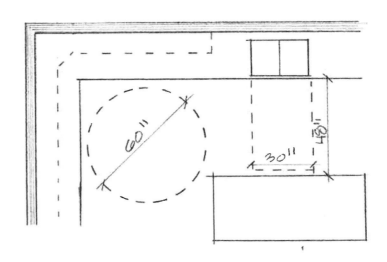

☑ ALWAYS PROVIDE CLEAR FLOOR SPACE OF 30" x 48" FOR SINK, COOKTOP AND WORK AREA.

☑ WHEN CREATING YOUR LAYOUT, THINK ABOUT THE DIRECTION OF APPROACH. A PERSON COULD BE APPROACHING FROM THE FRONT OR SIDE AND THIS WILL AFFECT THE POSITION OF THE CLEAR FLOOR SPACE

☑ BE SURE TO PROVIDE A 60" RADIUS WHERE TURNING IS NECESSARY

☑ YOU CAN FIND COMPLETE GUIDELINES AND STANDARDS FOR ADA REQUIREMENTS IN MANY CODES & STANDARDS BOOKS

KITCHEN APPLIANCES

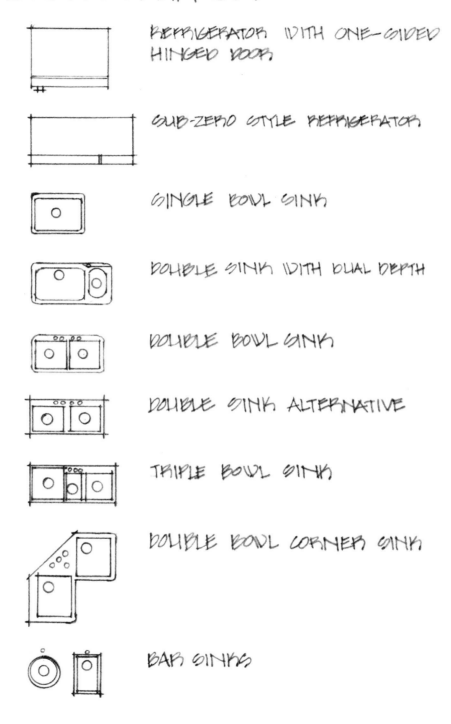

REFRIGERATOR WITH ONE-SIDED HINGED DOOR

SUB-ZERO STYLE REFRIGERATOR

SINGLE BOWL SINK

DOUBLE SINK WITH DUAL DEPTH

DOUBLE BOWL SINK

DOUBLE SINK ALTERNATIVE

TRIPLE BOWL SINK

DOUBLE BOWL CORNER SINK

BAR SINKS

KITCHEN APPLIANCES CONTINUED

 GAS COOKTOP

 GAS COOKTOP WITH CENTER DOWNDRAFT

 ELECTRIC RANGE WITH DOWN DRAFT

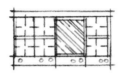 SIX-BURNER GAS COOKTOP WITH GRIDDLE

 GAS RANGE WITH DOOR HANDLE

 GRILL - DOWNDRAFT STYLE

 SINGLE COOK STATION - GAS

THERE ARE AS MANY COOKTOP
AND RANGE DESIGNS AS YOU CAN
IMAGINE AND DRAW.

EXAMPLE KITCHEN PLAN

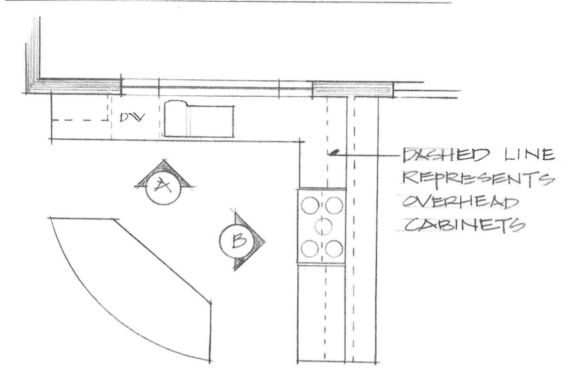

DW

A

B

DASHED LINE
REPRESENTS
OVERHEAD
CABINETS

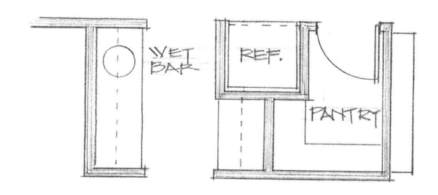

WET BAR

REF.

PANTRY

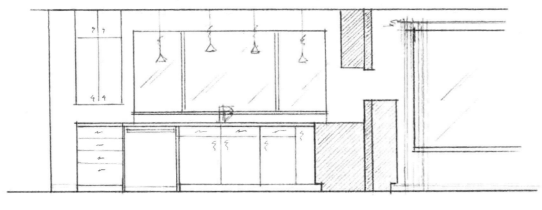

(A) SOUTH ELEVATION - KITCHEN

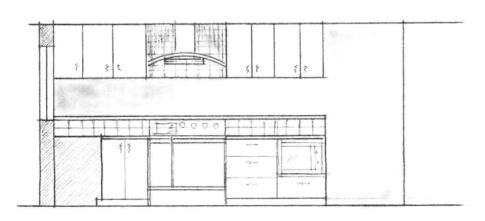

(B) WEST ELEVATION - KITCHEN

NOTICE THAT CONTEMPORARY KITCHENS
ARE DRAWN WITH LESS PANEL DETAIL.
THE DRAWING IS MORE CLEAN LINED.

KITCHEN ELEVATIONS

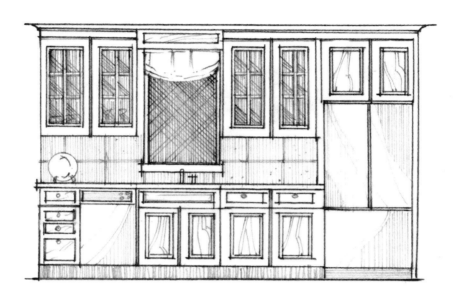

KITCHEN ELEVATIONS ARE USED TO SHOW DESIGN DETAILS, THE CABINET STYLE AND DESIGN STYLE OF THE AREA.

KITCHEN ELEVATIONS ARE GENERALLY IN HALF-INCH SCALE IN ORDER TO SHOW MORE DETAIL.

YOU CAN SHOW DETAILS OF THE FOLLOWING:
  WINDOWS
  WINDOW COVERINGS
  CABINET STYLE
  BACK-SPLASH DESIGN
  MOLDING
  SPECIAL EFFECTS

BATHS/RESTROOMS

Bathrooms today are often designed to have a spa atmosphere with large walk-in showers with benches, soaking tubs, and even saunas in some cases. Residential bathrooms are also being designed so that people can age in place. Adding features such as curb-less showers and bracing behind the walls for future grab bars will allow people to stay in their home if they become wheelchair bound. This chapter will show you almost everything you need to know to draw the details in your bath. Several basic layouts and details of how to draw fixtures are shown. Bathrooms can be as simple or as complex as the designer chooses to make them. The drawings will follow this simplicity or complexity. This chapter merely gives you the basis of possible layout spaces and details of how to draw the fixtures.

TYPICAL BATH LAYOUTS

TYPICAL BATH LAYOUTS CONTINUED

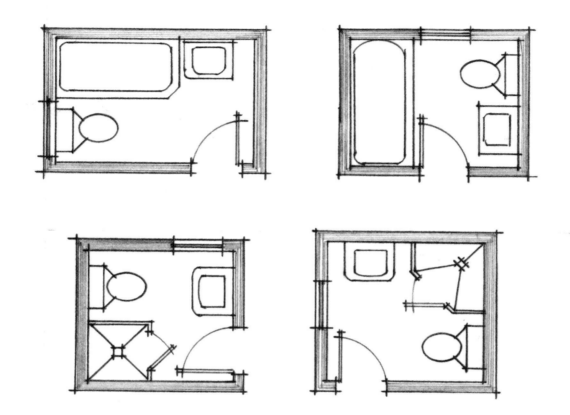

BATHROOMS

TOILETS CAN BE DRAWN WITH A TEMPLATE
BUT LOOK MUCH BETTER DRAWN ARTISTICALLY.

TEMPLATES

TOILETS DRAWN WITHOUT TEMPLATES

SHOWERS CAN BE SIMPLY DRAWN OR DRAWN
WITH MORE DETAIL TO SHOW TILE DESIGN.

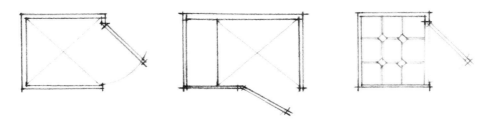

BATHTUBS NEED TO BE DRAWN WITH
MORE THAN A SINGLE LINE.

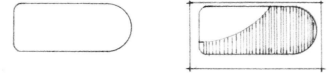

ADD SHADOWS

MORE TUB & SHOWER TECHNIQUES

TUB ENCLOSURE WITH SHOWER CURTAIN

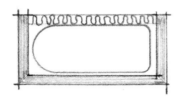

TUB ENCLOSURE WITH SLIDING DOORS

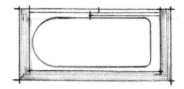

TUB ENCLOSURE WITH FRONT EXTENSION

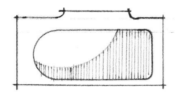

CORNER SHOWER

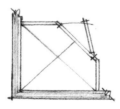

WALK-IN SHOWER

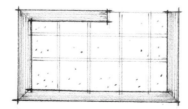

PLANNING FOR A BARRIER FREE RESTROOM

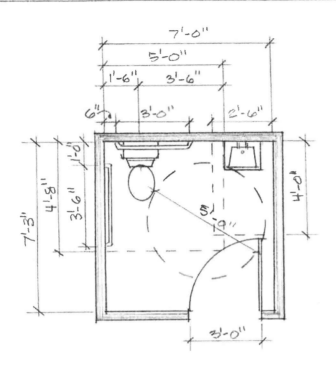

- THE ABOVE PLAN GIVES YOU THE BASIC DIMENSIONS TO DESIGN THE LAYOUT FOR A COMMERCIAL ADA RESTROOM

- YOU CAN ALSO USE THE INFORMATION ON GRAB BARS AND CLEAR FLOOR SPACE TO DESIGN VARIATIONS IN LAYOUT AND TO DESIGN A BARRIER FREE RESIDENTIAL BATHROOM

- PROVIDE 3'-0" DOOR FOR ENTRY

- DOOR SWING CANNOT INTERSECT WITH THE CLEAR FLOOR SPACE IN FRONT OF THE TOILET OR SINK

- PROVIDE GRAB BARS BESIDE & BEHIND TOILET

- SPECIFY SINK WITH OPEN AREA BELOW

- ITEMS ON WALLS SUCH AS PAPER TOWEL DISPENSER MUST BE MOUNTED WITHIN REACH (48" MAXIMUM)

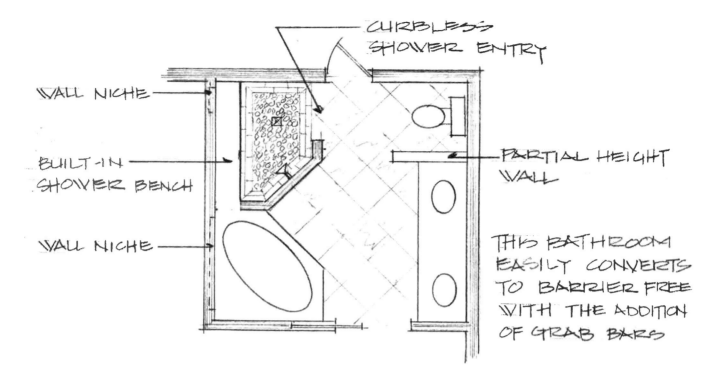

CURBLESS SHOWER ENTRY

WALL NICHE

BUILT-IN SHOWER BENCH

WALL NICHE

PARTIAL HEIGHT WALL

THIS BATHROOM EASILY CONVERTS TO BARRIER FREE WITH THE ADDITION OF GRAB BARS

EXAMPLE MASTER BATH

ELEVATION @ TUB/SHOWER

ELEVATION @ VANITY

TYPICAL COMMERCIAL RESTROOM

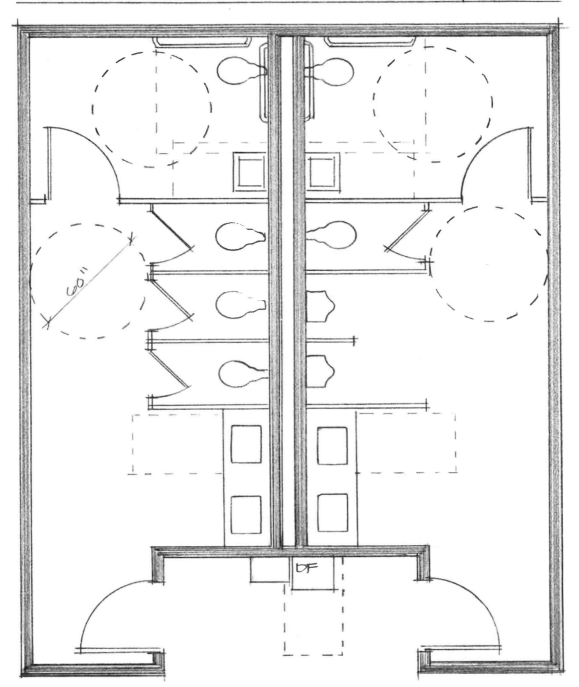

NOTE THE 60" ADA TURNING RADIUS AND THE CLEAR FLOOR SPACE IN FRONT OF SINK, TOILET & DRINKING FOUNTAIN.

CHAPTER ten

Process Drawings

Before drafting any space (commercial or residential), it is important to explore space planning options during the design development phase of a project. As interior designers, we are often hired to help with renovations or work with our commercial clients to design the layout for their tenant space. It is important to note that we can design anything with non-load-bearing walls (sometimes referred to as partitions). If we are working on a project that involves load-bearing walls, we need to work with an architect or engineer. During the programming phase, we gather everything the client needs as well as the codes that will apply to the project. This chapter will show you how to create bubble and block diagrams to explore adjacency needs and space-planning options. Examples of commercial space plans will also be shown.

BUBBLE TO BLOCK DIAGRAMMING TO FINAL PLAN

There are many books available on design process and space planning. Bubble diagrams are used to graphically represent the client needs and the adjacency requirements. A bubble diagram does not relate to the building layout. For very small projects, this step seems unimportant, but in large commercial spaces it is imperative. Imagine space planning a 20,000 square foot space with many needs. Once you understand the client needs and the adjacency requirements, you are ready to explore the layout within the base plan. Block plans take the bubble one step further and are used to explore multiple ways to lay out the given space. It is important to block out realistic square footage for each given space. Using grid paper under your plan can help you block spaces with adequate square footage.

Here is a list of helpful hints to keep in mind when you are space planning:

- Before beginning your block plans, always study the base plan. Look for the locations of columns and the spacing of window mullions.
- Walls must align with the window mullions.
- Pay attention to any plumbing restrictions.
- Corridor/circulation should be about 25 percent of total square footage. Do not waste space with unnecessary corridors.
- Minimum corridor width:
  - Residential—36"
  - Commercial—44" (60" recommended)
  - Healthcare—96"
- Do not create dead-end corridors more than 20' long in non-sprinkled spaces or 50' in sprinkled spaces (I recommend not exceeding 20' regardless). Creating loop circulation will help limit dead ends.
- All corridor intersections require the 60" turning radius.
- Plan perimeter of space first.
- Lay out locations of largest spaces first.
- Make sure all doors in the direction of means of egress swing out. Doors must also swing out in rooms with more than 49 occupants.
- Make sure that you provided the 12"/18" push/pull clearance at all doors (refer to "Typical Door Placement" example in Chapter 3).
- When possible, group plumbing together for efficiency and cost savings.
- With each block plan, evaluate the path of travel and means of egress.

In the following pages you will find two examples from bubble to block to plan.

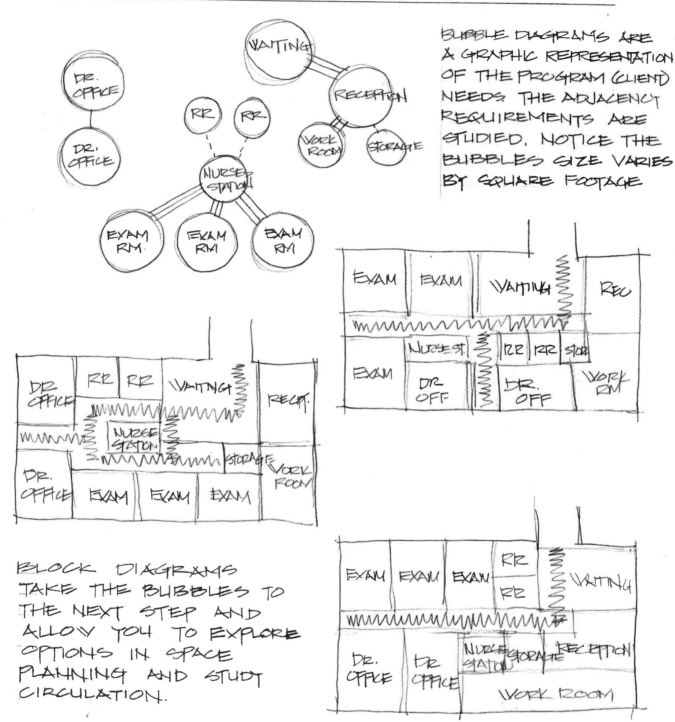

BUBBLE DIAGRAMS ARE A GRAPHIC REPRESENTATION OF THE PROGRAM (CLIENT) NEEDS THE ADJACENCY REQUIREMENTS ARE STUDIED. NOTICE THE BUBBLES SIZE VARIES BY SQUARE FOOTAGE

BLOCK DIAGRAMS TAKE THE BUBBLES TO THE NEXT STEP AND ALLOW YOU TO EXPLORE OPTIONS IN SPACE PLANNING AND STUDY CIRCULATION.

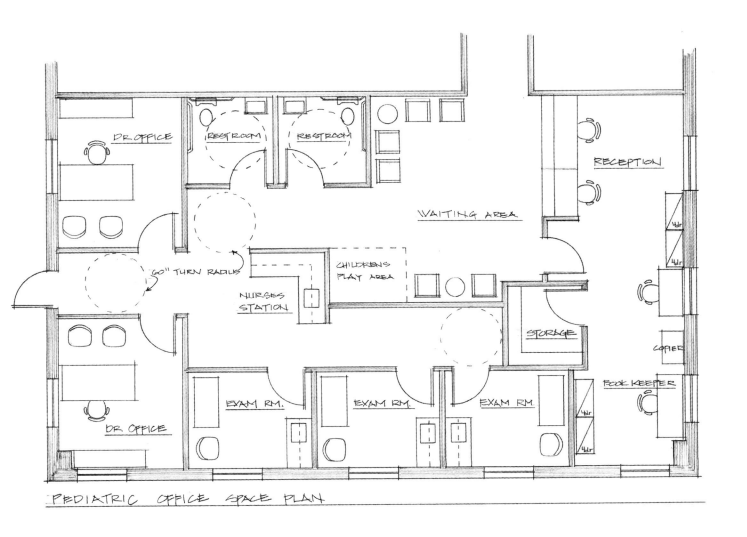

DR. OFFICE

RESTROOM

RESTROOM

WAITING AREA

RECEPTION

60" TURN RADIUS

NURSES STATION

CHILDRENS PLAY AREA

STORAGE

COPIER

BOOK KEEPER

DR OFFICE

EXAM RM.

EXAM RM.

EXAM RM.

PEDIATRIC OFFICE SPACE PLAN

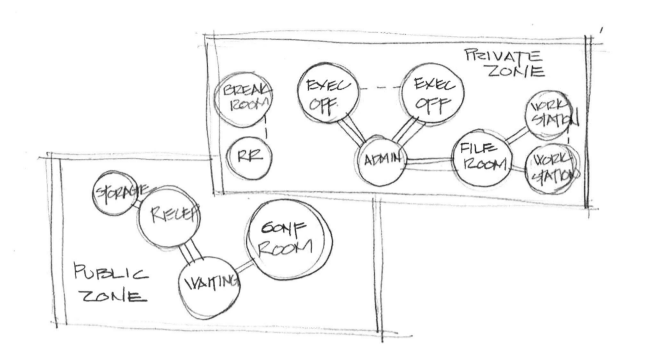

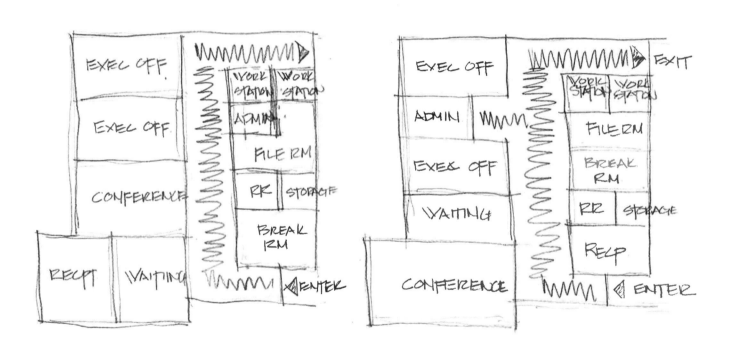

EXAMPLE #2   BUBBLE   TO   BLOCK   DIAGRAMMING

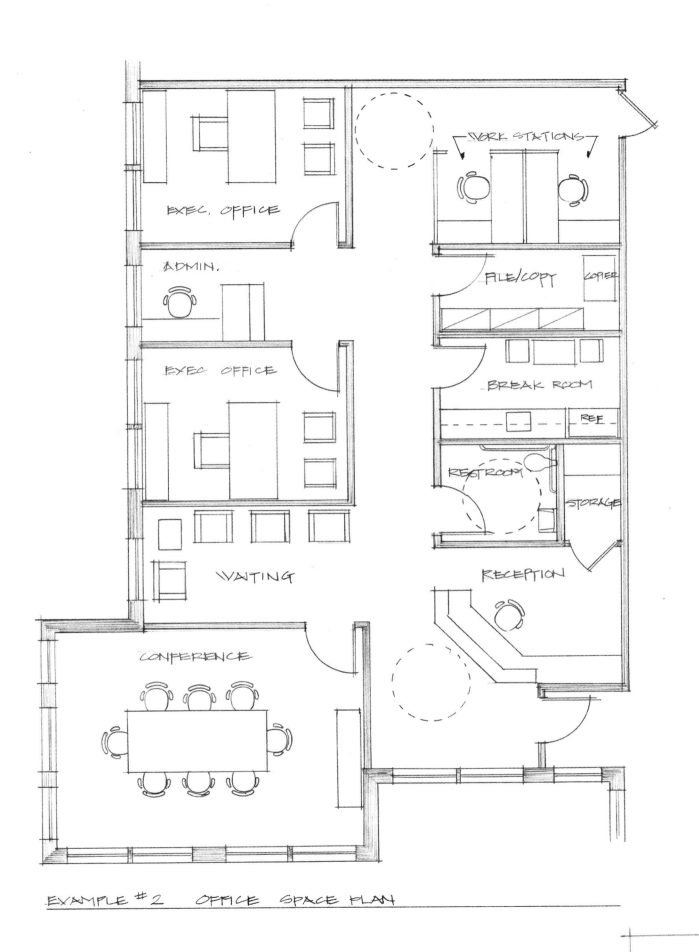

EXAMPLE #2   OFFICE   SPACE PLAN

Within the floor plan the following labels appear: EXEC. OFFICE, ADMIN., EXEC. OFFICE, WAITING, CONFERENCE, WORK STATIONS, FILE/COPY, COPIER, BREAK ROOM, REF., RESTROOM, STORAGE, RECEPTION

CHAPTER eleven

Custom Millwork

One of the most exciting parts of design is when you get the opportunity to create something unique. Custom millwork includes any built-in cabinetry, reception desks, etc. In historic preservation, millwork will include any woodworking such as paneling, molding, stair railing, fireplace surrounds, etc. Much of our custom detailing will use wood but may also use a variety of other materials. As interior designers, we provide our clients and the fabricators with plans, elevations, and section drawings to communicate our design intent. This chapter will give an overview of conventional woodworking construction and example drawings.

SHOP DRAWINGS

As an interior designer, you will be working with different fabricators to construct the custom elements you design. Once your client has approved the design, you will prepare detailed drawings that effectively communicate your design intent to the millwork shop. These drawings will include a carefully dimensioned plan view, elevations of all exposed sides of the piece, and section drawings through several places in the millwork. With thorough drawings you can avoid confusion and costly mistakes. Once you have submitted your drawings to the fabricator, they will provide you with their shop drawings for approval. It is important to review the shop drawings carefully to make sure that the materials and the design intent are intact before they construct the custom millwork.

CONVENTIONAL FLUSH CONSTRUCTION WITH FACE FRAME

☑ ALL DOOR & DRAWER FACES ARE FLUSH WITH THE FACE OF THE CABINET

SOFFIT
FACE FRAME
DRAWER LOCK JOINT
FACE FRAME
FLUSH DRAWER

(A) ELEVATION @ CABINETRY   (B) SECTION

FLUSH OVERLAY CONSTRUCTION

- CLEAN CONTEMPORARY LOOK
- ONLY DOOR & DRAWER FACES ARE VISIBLE FROM THE FRONT VIEW (ELEVATION)
- CRAFTSMANSHIP IS VERY IMPORTANT AS ALL COMPONENTS MUST BE ALIGNED FOR CONTINUITY.

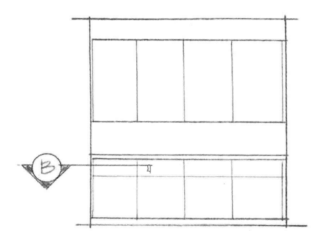

A ELEVATION @ CABINETRY

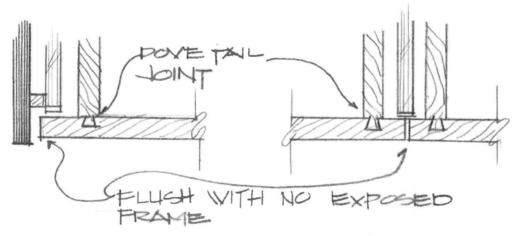

DOVE TAIL JOINT

FLUSH WITH NO EXPOSED FRAME

B SECTION @ DRAWERS

REVEAL OVERLAY CONSTRUCTION

■ THIS CONSTRUCTION STYLE CREATES A REVEAL BETWEEN DRAWER AND DOORS. THE REVEAL SIZE AND DIRECTION CAN BE VARIED. FOR EXAMPLE YOU MAY WANT TO DESIGN WITH A HORIZONTAL EMPHASIS.

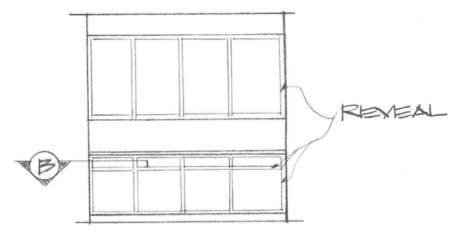

REVEAL

Ⓐ ELEVATION @ CABINETRY

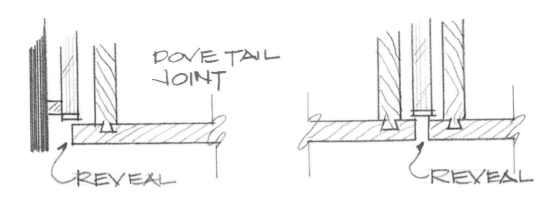

DOVETAIL JOINT

REVEAL

REVEAL

Ⓑ SECTION @ DRAWERS

TYPICAL JOINERY

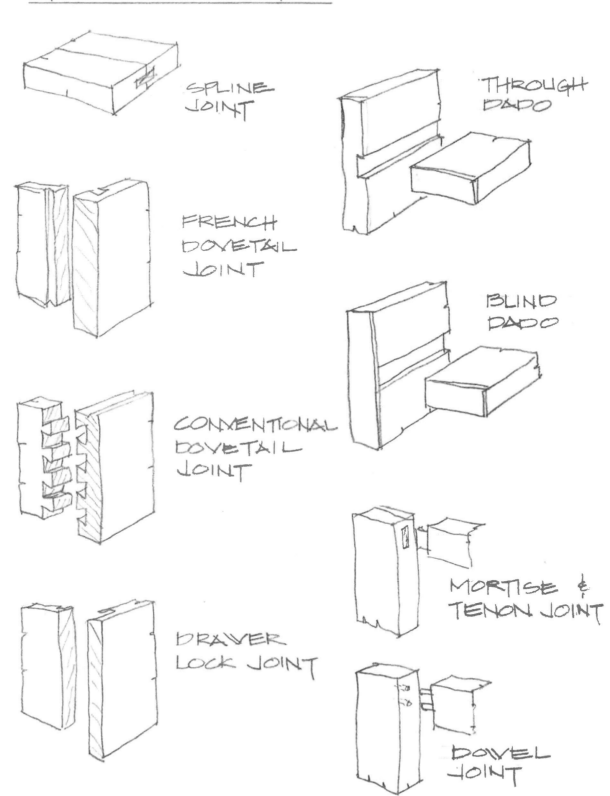

SPLINE JOINT

THROUGH DADO

FRENCH DOVETAIL JOINT

BLIND DADO

CONVENTIONAL DOVETAIL JOINT

MORTISE & TENON JOINT

DRAWER LOCK JOINT

DOVEL JOINT

DOOR & DRAWER DETAILS ARE IMPORTANT IN THE DESIGN OF MILLWORK AND WILL AFFECT THE AESTHETIC. A SOLID PANEL DOOR CAN GIVE A SIMPLE, CLEAN, CONTEMPORARY APPEARANCE AND CAN BE FINISHED IN PLASTIC LAMINATE, WOOD VENEER, OR SOLID WOOD. PANELED DOOR DETAILS CAN BE DESIGNED ACCORDING TO THE STYLE AND PREFERENCE.

PANELED DOOR DETAILS

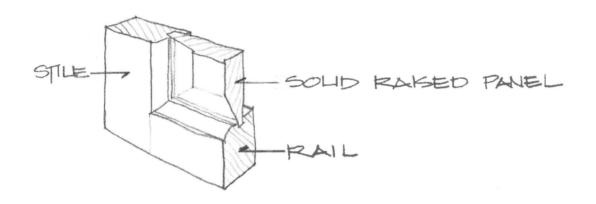

STILE — SOLID RAISED PANEL
RAIL

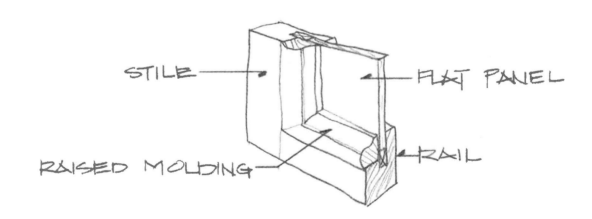

STILE — FLAT PANEL
RAISED MOLDING — RAIL

CUSTOM MILLWORK

WHEN PRESENTING TO A CLIENT OR SENDING DRAWINGS OUT FOR BID YOU WILL WANT TO INCLUDE A PLAN VIEW, ELEVATIONS AND A SECTION DRAWING. IF THE DESIGN IS COMPLEX IT MAY REQUIRE SEVERAL ELEVATIONS, SECTIONS, AND A PARALINE DRAWING.

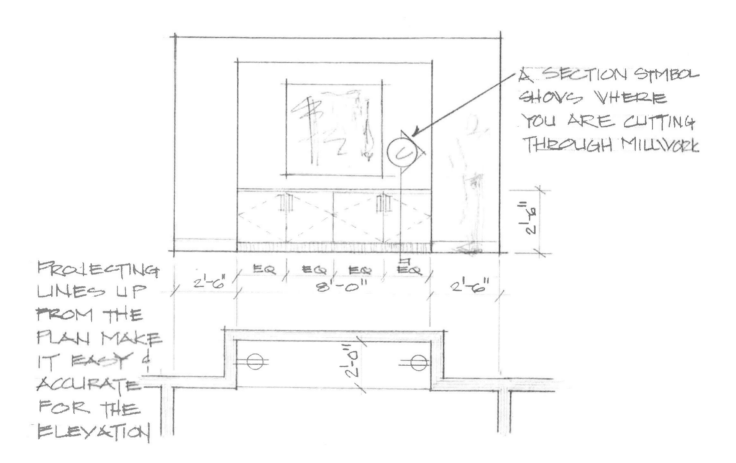

A SECTION SYMBOL SHOWS WHERE YOU ARE CUTTING THROUGH MILLWORK

2'-6"

PROJECTING LINES UP FROM THE PLAN MAKE IT EASY & ACCURATE FOR THE ELEVATION

2'-6" EQ EQ EQ EQ 2'-6"

8'-0"

2'-0"

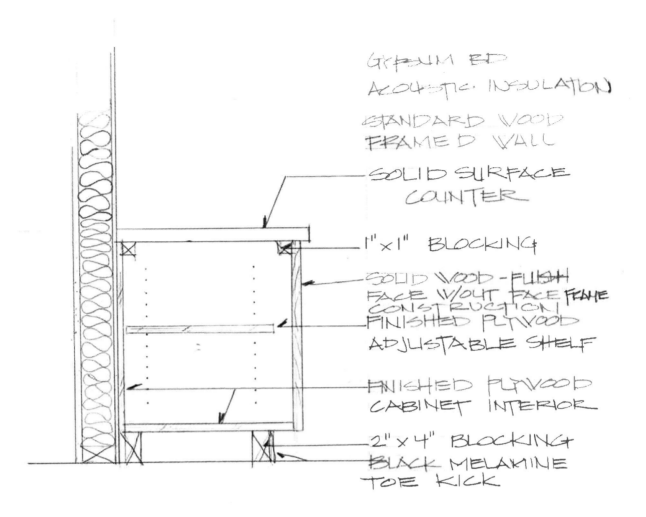

GYPSUM BD
ACOUSTIC INSULATION
STANDARD WOOD
FRAMED WALL

SOLID SURFACE
COUNTER

1"×1" BLOCKING

SOLID WOOD - FLUSH
FACE W/OUT FACE FRAME
CONSTRUCTION
FINISHED PLYWOOD
ADJUSTABLE SHELF

FINISHED PLYWOOD
CABINET INTERIOR

2"×4" BLOCKING
BLACK MELAMINE
TOE KICK

C SECTION @ CONFERENCE RM. CAB.
SCALE 1"=1'-0"

SECTION DRAWINGS ARE DONE TO
COMMUNICATE THE OVERALL CONSTRUCTION
AND MATERIALS OF THE MILLWORK. THEY
ALSO SHOW THE INTERIOR OF THE CABINET.
IT IS AS THOUGH YOU ARE SLICING THROUGH
THE PIECE AND PULLING A SECTION APART
TO LOOK AT THE STRUCTURAL MATERIALS.

CUSTOM MILLWORK

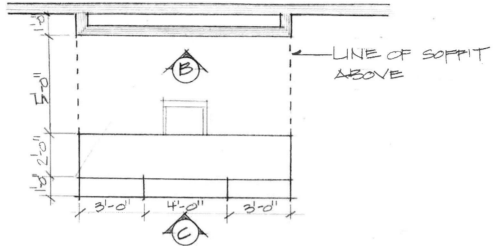

LINE OF SOFFIT ABOVE

3'-0"   4'-0"   3'-0"

Ⓐ PLAN VIEW @ RECEPTION DESK
SCALE 1/4"=1'-0"

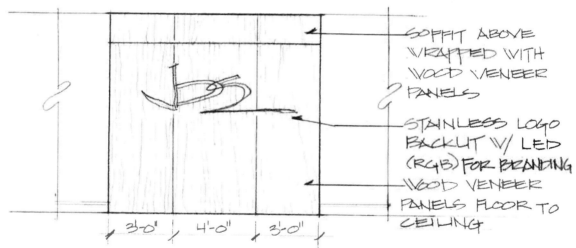

SOFFIT ABOVE WRAPPED WITH WOOD VENEER PANELS

STAINLESS LOGO BACKLIT W/ LED (RGB) FOR BRANDING

WOOD VENEER PANELS FLOOR TO CEILING

3'-0"   4'-0"   3'-0"

Ⓑ ELEVATION @ WALL BEHIND DESK
SCALE 1/4"=1'-0"

CUSTOM MILLWORK

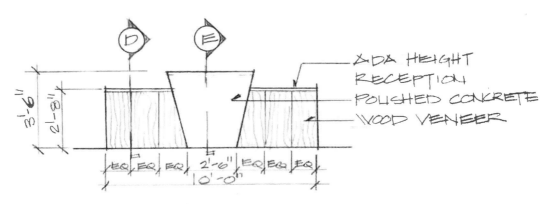

3'-6"
2'-8"

ADA HEIGHT
RECEPTION
POLISHED CONCRETE
WOOD VENEER

EQ | EQ | EQ | 2'-6" | EQ | EQ | EQ
10'-0"

C ELEVATION @ RECEPTION DESK
SCALE 1/4"=1'-0"

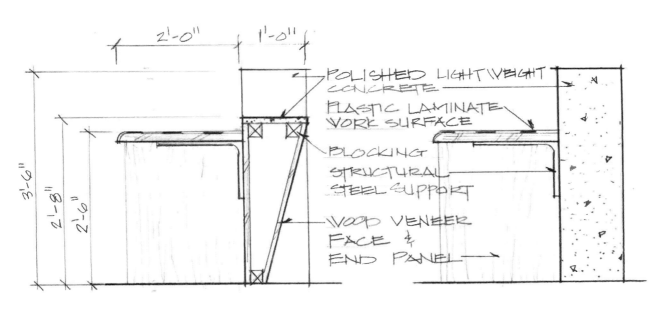

2'-0"   1'-0"

POLISHED LIGHTWEIGHT
CONCRETE

PLASTIC LAMINATE
WORK SURFACE

BLOCKING

STRUCTURAL
STEEL SUPPORT

WOOD VENEER
FACE &
END PANEL

3'-6"
2'-8"
2'-6"

D SECTION @ ADA COUNTER
SCALE 3/4"=1'-0"

E SECTION @ COUNTER
SCALE 3/4"=1'

CHAPTER twelve

Quick Sketching

Quick sketching is another form of drafting and helps us quickly generate ideas during the design process. It is also helpful to be able to sketch to scale to solve problems that arise on the job site. Quick sketches can also be used during a client meeting or when communicating ideas to our co-workers. When quickly sketching plans and elevations, it can be helpful to use grid paper as a guideline. Most designers like to use trace paper (also known as trash) to loosely explore design ideas. Sketching takes practice. When sketching for ideation, don't be afraid to be a little sloppy. With practice, even your loose drawings on trace paper can become preliminary drawings that you might show a client to verify that you are headed in the right direction. Most junior designers will be working under senior designers and architects and will need to communicate with quick sketching before proceeding to final drawings. In this chapter, you will see some examples of loose sketches.

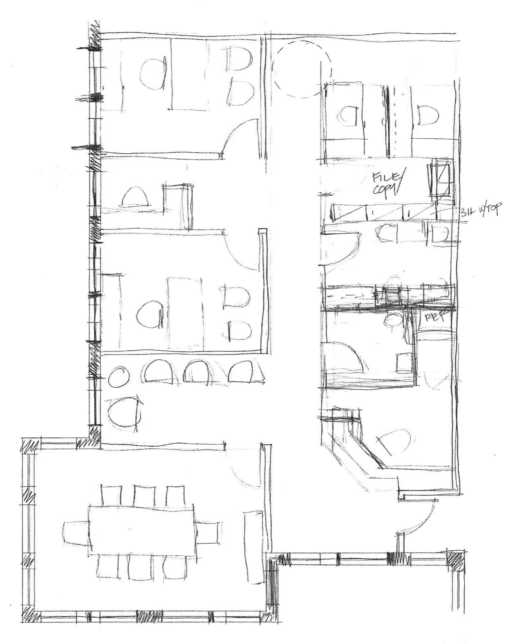

FILE/
COPY

31L W/TOP

REF

EXAMPLE OF QUICK SKETCHING PRIOR TO FINALIZING
PLAN. USING GRID PAPER TO WORK OUT SPACE PLANNING
DETAILS

PENCIL SKETCHES

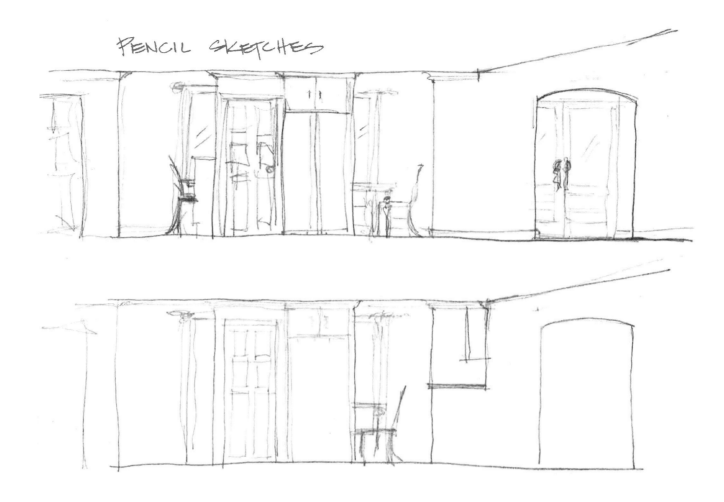

☑ QUICK SKETCHING CAN HELP YOU EXPLORE
OPTIONS WHEN YOU ARE IN THE DESIGN PHASE
IT IS HELPFUL FOR BOTH SPACE PLANNING
AND WORKING OUT DETAILS IN ELEVATIONS
AND SECTIONS BEFORE YOU PROCEED TO
YOUR DRAFTED DRAWINGS. HERE ARE A FEW
HINTS WHEN SKETCHING.
☑ YOU CAN USE GRID PAPER TO HELP WITH SCALE
☑ WORK QUICKLY ON TRACE PAPER
☑ NEVER ERASE - JUST LAYER TRACE PAPER
☑ USE PENCIL, INK, OR MARKER (I PREFER
A SHARPIE FOR LOOSE SKETCHING.

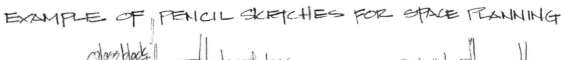

EXAMPLE OF PENCIL SKETCHES FOR SPACE PLANNING

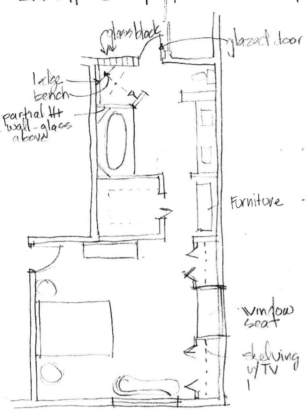

glass block

glazed door

large bench

partial ht wall - glass above

Furniture

Window seat

shelving w/TV

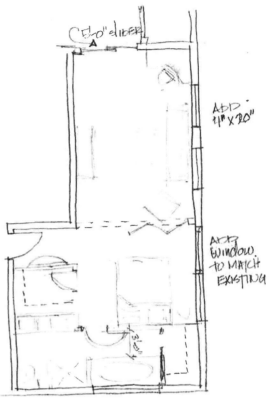

CL 5'-0" dider A

ADD 11" x 20"

ADD window to match existing

OPTION 1

☐ ADD GLASS BLOCK
    1 DOOR

☐ RELOCATE DOOR, CLOSETS
    ADD WINDOW SEAT

☐ ADVANTAGES
    • BATH ACCESS TO POOL
    • MORE LF CLOSET SPACE
    • MORE ECONOMICAL

☐ DISADVANTAGES
    • LITTLE VIEW TO POOL/CANAL
    • NO OFFICE/LOUNGE SPACE

OPTION 2

☐ RELOCATE PLUMBING
    CLOSETS

☐ ADD 3 WINDOWS
    1 SLIDING DOOR

☐ REQUIRE ELECTRICAL
    HVAC DUCT WORK
    REDONE.

☐ ADVANTAGES
    • VIEW FROM MASTER SUITE
    • MORE LIVING/OFFICE SPACE
    • MORE NATURAL LIGHT

☐ DISADVANTAGES
    • COST
    • LESS CLOSET SPACE

QUICK ELEVATION - IN INK

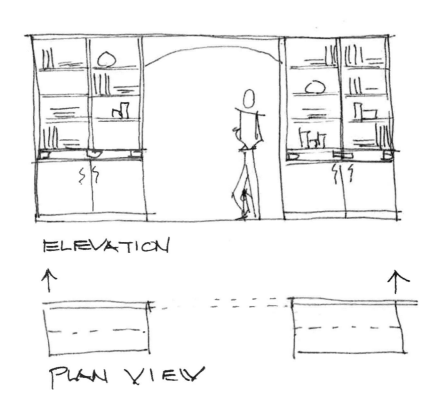

ELEVATION

PLAN VIEW

CONCEPT DEVELOPMENT SKETCHING

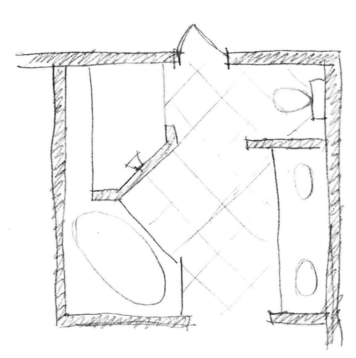

DON'T BE AFRAID TO BE A LITTLE SLOPPY
IN YOUR LOOSE IDEATION SKETCHING.

QUICK SKETCHING
IN 3-D WILL HELP
YOU VISUALIZE THE TOTAL SPACE

QUICK ELEVATION -
INK & PENCIL

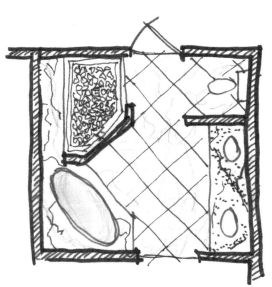

LOOSE IDEATION SKETCHING
INK & MARKER

CHAPTER TWELVE

QUICK ELEVATION - INK & MARKER

CHAPTER thirteen

Putting It All Together

Now that you have learned about many of the components of hand drafting, let us focus on presenting your drawings. There are two ways you will present your drawings. The first way is to create presentation sheets that are used to sell your ideas to your clients. These will include plans and elevations that have added materials and shade and shadow. You may add color to those drawings to create beautiful colored renderings. Oftentimes these types of drawings will be matted for presentation boards. The second way you will present your drawings is in a set. These are often called construction documents, as they will be used to work with the contractors to get the project completed. There are many books on construction documentation. This chapter will cover title blocks, sheet layouts, symbols, and the different components you may include in your set of drawings. Regardless of the size and type of project, it is important to have a complete and clear set of documents that allows the project to proceed to completion with minimal complications and misunderstandings.

Below is a list of components and a description that may be included in a set of documents.

- **Title Block**—Commercial construction drawings can be lengthy (up to as many as 200 sheets). To avoid confusion, each sheet within the set should have a title block. The amount of information included in a title block can vary.

- **Cover Sheet**—In some cases an optional cover sheet is used. This sheet will have a perspective drawing of the space. It might also simply show the client's name and project address. All design firms have a standard format for documenting and organizing their projects. It may vary slightly from what is presented in this chapter.

- **Index Sheet**—Just as every sheet should have its own title block, every set of construction drawings should have its own index sheet. The purpose of the index sheet is to avoid confusion and assist the user in reading the documents. Most firms will have a standard index sheet that is used for all projects. The only thing that would change on it is the index of drawings. An index sheet may include Material Indications, Architectural Symbols, Reference Symbols, General Notes, etc. An index sheet will always include an Index of Drawings that is similar to a table of contents.

- **Furniture Plan**—Some firms will put this plan first and others will put it last, as the furniture is the last to be installed in a project. The furniture plan shows the location of all furniture and equipment. All furniture will be tagged and will relate back to furniture specifications. Furniture specifications are generally placed in a binder with all furniture and finish specifications.

- **Demolition Plan**—A demolition plan is necessary for renovation work. This plan shows the location of all walls/doors to be removed. Sometimes this can be included on the partition plan.

- **Partition Plan**—The partition plan shows the location of all walls, doors, and windows. It will be dimensioned, and partition types will be tagged to relate to the partition sections. This will show what partitions are fire rated, have acoustic insulation, are partial height, etc. The doors will also be tagged and will relate to the door schedule.

- **Electrical Plan**—The electrical plan will show the locations and types of all telephone, data, and electrical outlets. As an interior designer, you will just be providing the locations for these items. Dimension the location of any critical placements. Always place a symbols legend on the sheet with the electrical plan if possible. The engineers working on the project will finalize the MEP drawings that accompany the set of drawings.

- **Reflected Ceiling Plan**—This plan shows the locations and types of all ceiling materials, ceiling-mounted lighting fixtures, and other elements on the ceiling. It is as if you have placed a mirror on the floor to see what is in the ceiling plane. If a space has lighting mounted on the walls, floor, etc., you may choose to label the plan as a lighting plan. A true reflected ceiling plan only shows the elements that are on the ceiling.

- **Finish Plan**—In spaces with complex placement of different flooring materials and patterns and wall materials, a finish plan can be a helpful tool in communicating the design intent. The material tags will relate to the finish schedules and specifications.

- **Detail Sheets**—A series of detail sheets generally follow the plan drawings. These sheets provide detail drawings addressing the construction of partitions, cabinetry custom millwork, ceiling details, and any other items for which the design intent is not communicated in the plan drawings. It is important for these details to be clearly dimensioned and labeled.

- **Schedules and Specifications**—A complete set of schedules and specifications will accompany any set of construction documents. These schedules and specifications may be found throughout the documents on the sheets that they relate to, in a separate binder, or on a schedule sheet. Some common schedules and specifications include:
  - Lighting Schedule
  - Furniture Schedule
  - Material Schedule
  - Door Schedule
  - Hardware Schedule
  - Furniture Specifications
  - Finish Schedule
  - Finish Specifications

TITLE BLOCKS

DESIGN FIRM INFO.	DESIGN FIRM NAME, ADDRESS, LOGO ARE GENERALLY FOUND IN THE TOP SECTION OF THE TITLE BLOCK
SEAL	PROVIDE SPACE FOR AN ARCHITECTURAL OR INTERIOR SEAL. SOME STATES ALLOW INTERIOR DESIGNERS TO STAMP DRAWINGS FOR NON-STRUCTURAL
ISSUE: REVISIONS	THE ISSUE AND REVISIONS GIVES A PLACE TO RECORD DATES OF ISSUE AND REVISIONS.
CLIENT APP.	ALWAYS PROVIDE A SPACE FOR CLIENT APPROVAL SIGNATURE
CLIENT INFO. ADDRESS	PROJECT INFORMATION INCLUDING ADDRESS IS IMPORTANT AS IT WILL AFFECT ZONING & CODES
SHEET TITLE	SHEET TITLE REFERS TO WHAT IS ON THE SHEET (EXAMPLE - FLOOR PLAN)
SCALE DRAWN BY DATE	SCALE: IF MORE THAN ONE SCALE ON SHEET STATE "AS NOTED" DRAWN BY & DATE USE INITIALS AND DATE DRAWN OR FINALIZED
SHEET # A1 3 OF 12	SHEET # IS ALWAYS AT BOTTOM RIGHT OF SHEET. IT IS IMPORTANT TO NOTE TOTAL SHEETS IN SET TO AVOID INCOMPLETE SETS OF CD'S AT THE JOB SITE.

DEPENDING ON THE SIZE AND SCALE OF THE PROJECT YOUR FIRM MAY HAVE A SIMPLIFIED TITLE BLOCK SUCH AS THE EXAMPLE BELOW

JDSD J·D·S·DESIGN 149735	NASH RESIDENCE 7432 LINCOLN DR. WASHINGTON D.C.	Sheet Title FLOOR PLAN	Scale 1/4"=1'-0" Drawn By JDS Date 5-4-2019	Sheet Number A1 2 of 5

EXAMPLE COVER/INDEX SHEET

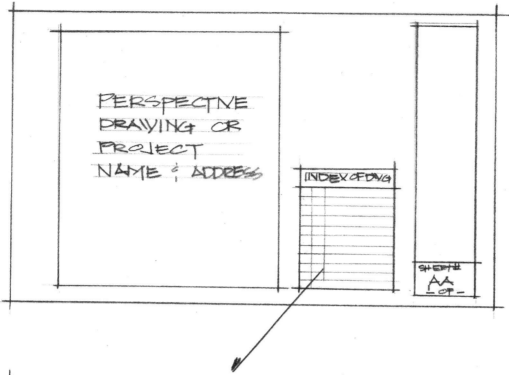

PERSPECTIVE
DRAWING OR
PROJECT
NAME & ADDRESS

INDEX OF DWG

SHEET #
AA
_ OF _

INDEX OF DRAWINGS

PG	SHT	TITLE
1	AA	INDEX/COVER SHEET
2	AB	SCHEDULES / REF. SYMBOLS
3	A1	PARTITION PLAN
4	A2	ELECTRICAL PLAN
5	A3	REFLECTED CEILING PLAN
6	F1	FURNITURE PLAN
7	D1	SECTIONS OF PARTITIONS
8	D2	DETAILS OF REST ROOMS
9	D3	DETAILS OF RECEPTION DESK
10	D4	MISCELLANEOUS DETAILS

THINK OF THE INDEX LIKE A TABLE OF CONTENTS. IT ALLOWS THE READER TO QUICKLY FIND WHAT THEY ARE LOOKING FOR. INDEX OF DRAWINGS CAN GET VERY LONG FOR LARGE PROJECTS WITH MANY SHEETS.

EXAMPLE TYPICAL PLAN SHEET

PLAN VIEW

NOTES

LEGEND

A1
_OF_

(A/AB) PLAN VIEW

(A/A1) DRAWING#

SHEET#

ELEVATION SYMBOL USED IN PLAN

SECTION SYMBOL

EXAMPLE TYPICAL DETAIL SHEET

ENLARGED PLAN OF SPECIFIC AREA, WITH DIMENSIONS & MATERIALS

ELEVATION WITH DIMENSION & MATERIAL NOTES

(A/D1) DIMENSIONED PLAN

(B/D1) ELEVATION

(E/P1)

SECTION SHOWING DETAIL

(C/D1) ELEVATION

(D/D1) ELEV.

(E/D1) SECTION

SHEET#
D1
_OF_

REFERENCES

II—⬭ 3/D1	SECTION # / SHEET #	SECTION - USED ON PLANS AND ELEVATIONS
◁ 5/D2	ELEVATION # / SHEET #	ELEVATION - USED ON PLANS
◯ 1/D1	DRAWING # / SHEET #	DRAWING LABEL - USED ON ALL SHEETS
[1001]		ROOM #
⌂ A		DOOR TYPE - SYMBOL REFERS TO DOOR SCHEDULE
⬡ M		WALL FINISH - USED ON FINISH PLAN
C1 / CB	INDICATES FLOORING / INDICATES BASE	FLOOR FINISH - USED ON FINISH PLAN
—[5]		PARTITION TYPE

YOU WILL ALSO SEE LEGENDS THAT SHOW MATERIAL INDICATIONS AND ARCHITECTURAL SYMBOLS. ADDITIONAL SYMBOLS CAN BE FOUND IN MANY GRAPHIC STANDARDS BOOKS.

RECEPTACLE SYMBOLS

⊖	SINGLE RECEPTACLE - DEDICATED CIRCUIT
⊕	STANDARD DUPLEX GROUNDED RECEPTACLE
⊕	QUADRUPLEY RECEPTACLE - TWO GANG BOX WITH FOUR RECEPTACLES
⊕	TRIPLEX RECEPTACLE - TWO GANG BOX WITH THREE RECEPTACLES
⊖$_S$	DUPLEX RECEPTACLE WITH SWITCH
⊖$_{WP}$	WATERPROOF RECEPTACLE WITH COVER
▣	FLOOR DUPLEX OUTLET
⊖$_{GFI}$	GROUND FAULT INTERUPTER RECEPTACLE USED NEAR WATER SOURCES PER CODE
⊖	SPLIT WIRED DUPLEX RECEPTACLE - TOP CONTROLLED BY SWITCH, USED FOR LAMPS
⊖$_R$	RANGE RECEPTACLE 50 AMP 4 WIRE
⊖$_{CD}$	CLOTHS DRYER RECEPTACLE 30 AMP 4 WIRE
⊖$_S$	SINGLE RECEPTACLE WITH SWITCH
▣	FLOOR JUNCTION BOX
⊕	JUNCTION BOX
◁	TELEPHONE JACK
◀	DATA CONNECTION OUTLET

SWITCH SYMBOLS

$	SINGLE SWITCH - TURNS ON ONE OR MORE LIGHTS FROM ONE LOCATION
$3	3-WAY SWITCH - TURNS LIGHTS ON FROM TWO LOCATIONS (NEEDED FOR ROOMS W/ 2 DOORS)
$4	4-WAY SWITCH - USED TO TURN ON TWO 3-WAY SWITCHES FROM THREE LOCATIONS
$DM	DIMMER SWITCH - USED TO CONTROL INTENSITY OF LIGHT (NOT ALL TYPES OF LIGHT CAN DIM)
$3DM	THREE WAY DIMMER SWITCH - USED TO CONTROL LIGHT INTENSITY FROM TWO LOCATIONS
$OS	SWITCH WITH OCCUPANCY SENSOR - USED IN COMMERCIAL SPACES TO SAVE ENERGY
Ⓢ	CEILING PULL SWITCH - USED IN ATTICS AND CLOSETS
T	THERMOSTAT (NOTE MOUNTING HEIGHT PER CODE)

NOTE: ALWAYS NOTE MOUNTING HEIGHTS. SOME HEIGHTS ARE DICTATED BY CODE, OTHERS ARE THE DESIGNERS CHOICE. SWITCHES AND OUTLETS ARE MEASURED TO THE CENTER LINE A.F.F. (ABOVE FINISHED FLOOR)

LIGHTING - RCP SYMBOLS

⊕	SURFACE MOUNTED FIXTURE
○	RECESSED CAN FIXTURE
◑	WALL WASHER
○→	DIRECTIONAL CEILING MOUNTED FIXTURE
–○–	PENDANT (ALWAYS NOTE MOUNTING HEIGHT AFF)
▣	TROFFER - COME IN VARYING SIZES
⊏▭⊐	SURFACE MOUNTED LINEAR LIGHTING
▪▭▪	SUSPENDED LINEAR (NOTE MOUNTING HEIGHT AFF)
▵▵▵	TRACK LIGHTING
– – – –	COVE LIGHTING (ALWAYS PROVIDE DETAIL SECTION)
– ⋅ – ⋅	GRAZING FIXTURE
⊢○	WALL SCONCE (NOTE HEIGHT AFF TO ₵)
⊏○⊐	FLUORESCENT LIGHT
▷◁	UNDER CABINET LIGHT
Ⓢ	SMOKE DETECTOR
Ⓕ	FAN
Ⓕ⁄ₗ	FAN/LIGHT COMBINATION
⊗	EMERGENCY EXIT SIGN
▽▽	EMERGENCY LIGHTING
⊠	HVAC SUPPLY
◻	HVAC RETURN
◉	SPRINKLER

Glossary

Interior Design Drafting Terms

A

Accordion Doors Folding doors with narrow vertical panels that stack side by side

Alcove Indented opening off a wall, sometimes used for displaying art

Anthropometrics The comparison and study of human body measurements

Apron Horizontal trim under the sill of the interior window

Architect A professional who designs three-dimensional space and creates the floor plans and interior and exterior design

Architectural Elements The floors, ceilings, windows, doors, fireplaces, walls, cabinetry, and other fixtures or details that are built in an interior

Area Rug Type of rug that can define an area for conversation

ASID American Society of Interior Design

Attic Space between the ceiling and the roof

Awning Window Top hinging window that opens out

Axonometric Drawing Type of drawing that includes isometric, elevation, oblique, and plan oblique drawings; a single view drawing with all lines parallel and projected at an angle. Also referred to as paraline drawing.

B

Background Components of a drawing that take place in the space behind the center of interest

Backsplash Area behind a countertop, usually measuring 4" to 18" vertically

Balcony Deck above ground level, projecting from the interior or exterior

Baluster Small vertical component in the railing used between the top rail and the stair treads or bottom rail

Balustrade The railing formed by the newel post, baluster, and handrail

Bannister Handrail with supporting posts used beside a stairway

Barrier-Free Design Design approach with no physical obstacles or barriers, allowing free movement in the environment

Base Cabinets The lower segment of cabinets in kitchens or other rooms that support the countertops

Baseboard The finishing board of a variety of different materials that covers the area where the wall joins the floor

Batten Strip of wood or metal used to cover vertical joints between boards

Bay Window A window projecting away from the exterior of the building

Beadboard Wood paneling with vertical grooves milled so it looks like board and batten walls

Beam Horizontal structural member supporting a load

Bearing Wall A wall that supports a structural floor or roof load

Bifold Doors Doors that fold together to open

Black-Line Print A type of reproduction of drawings that has black lines on a gray background

Blueprints Floor plans printed in blue ink used for the construction of buildings

Board and Batten Siding technique that uses narrow strips of wood, called battens, placed evenly in a pattern over the wooden siding; a technique originally designed to hide the vertical cracks between the boards

Breast The front of the fireplace and chimney

Brown-Line Print Same as a black-line print, but the lines are brown; also known as a sepia print

Bubble Diagram The first step of programming where bubbles represent zones and areas where the spaces will be designed in proximity to one another

Building Code Federal, state, or local ruling laws that stipulate building safety and health requirements to help ensure the safety, health, and welfare of the general public during construction and occupancy

Bullnose 180-degree rounding of the edge of a material, usually on wood or stone. See also Nosing.

C

Cabinetry Fine finished woodworking

CAD/CADD Computer-aided drawing/computer-aided drafting and design

Capital The decorative top of a pillar or column

Casement A window frame that is hinged on the side

Casement Window A hinged window that opens outward

Casing Trim surrounding window and door openings

Cathedral Window An angular window set in the gable of a room with a slanted ceiling

Chair Rail A trim piece or molding attached to the wall at chair-back height, generally placed to protect the wall from damage from the back of the chair

Chandelier A decorative, ceiling-mounted luminaire, usually with several arms or branches for candles or lamps

Clerestory Window Window positioned near the top of a wall

Column Vertical structural or non-structural member

Combination Window A window with one section of stationary glass and the other a different type of window, like an awning

Compass Drafting instrument used to draw circles or curves

Concrete Mixture of gravel, sand, cement, and water

Construction Drawings See Working Drawings

Corbel Masonry or woodworking that is stepped out to protect the wall

Cross-Hatching A drawing technique used to create visual texture; using pencil or pen, superimposing the crossing of lines in opposite directions, usually X's done many times; this technique often is used in the poché of walls in a floor plan

Crown Molding Molding used where the ceiling meets the wall

D

Demolition Plan A drawing drafted to show elements of a project that are to be eliminated

Design Concept A design or an idea for a design to find the solution to a problem, pulling together different ideas to form a viable design

Detail Drawing Scale drawing that depicts in detail a specific feature of a design concept

Dimensions Numerical values used to indicate size and distance in a drawing

Door Jamb The vertical elements that form the inside of the door opening held together by a horizontal member

Door Stop An object or device used to hold a door open or closed, or to prevent a door from opening too widely

Double Action Door Door that swings both inward and outward

Double Glaze Window Two layers of glass set in a window to reduce heat flow in either direction

Double Hung Window A window having two vertically sliding sashes, each designed to close a different half of the window

Drafting Hand drawing of cabinetry, floor plans, elevations, reflected ceiling plans, and architectural details

Drafting Board Smooth board on which paper is placed for making drawings; often can be set at an incline

Drafting Brush A handled brush used to clean erasures from the drawing surface

Drafting Machine A drafting instrument designed much like a human arm

Drafting Table A multipurpose desk that can be used for any kind of drawing, writing, or impromptu sketching on a large sheet of paper; for reading a large-format book or other oversized documents; or for drafting precise technical illustrations

Dressing Artistic enhancement of a drawing to further clarify part of the design concept

Duplex Outlet Electrical receptacle capable of receiving two plugs

Dutch Door Door whose top portion opens and closes independently from its bottom portion

E **Eave** The lower edge of the roof that extends beyond the exterior wall

Electrical Plan A drafted scale drawing indicating the circuitry and location of electrical elements, including switches and outlets

Elevation A 2D drawing that is drawn to scale viewing a wall plane. Items in the room placed in front of the wall may also be shown in the drawing. An elevation includes the floor plane to the ceiling plane in 2D. You will not see the floor or ceiling but only the wall plane.

Erasing Shield A small metal template used to cover areas that are not going to be erased while showing the areas that will be erased

Ergonomics The study of human body movement and its relationship to the space in which it functions

F **Fascia** A horizontal board that is used to face a roof edge

Fenestration The design and placement of windows in a wall

Flagstone Type of flat stone used in landscaping and interiors for walkways and walls

Floor Plan Scaled drawing, typically drawn at ¼" to 1'-0" scale, indicating walls, windows, electrical outlets, furniture placement, etc.

French Curve A drafting tool used to draw irregular curves

French Doors Two doors closing against each other within a frame

G **Gambrel Roof** Ridged roof with two sloped sides, the lower slope having the steeper pitch

Ganging Term used to indicate installation of several outlets or switches next to each other

Guideline An exceptionally light line (often created with a 4H pencil) used for lining up lettering and numbers and used to form the basis for darker lines

H **Hardwood** Wood produced from broad-leafed trees or trees that lose their leaves, such as maple, birch, oak, and walnut

Head Room The space between the top of a finished floor and the lowest part of the floor above

Hearth Floor surface of a fireplace, either inside or in front of the fireplace; often raised and used for a seat

Heavy Line Weight A dark line (often made with an F pencil) used to indicate lines of primary importance in a drawing

Hopper Window Hinged at the bottom and opens outward

HVAC The abbreviation for heating, ventilation, air-conditioning units

I

Insulation Material used to hinder the transfer of cold, heat, and/or sound from one area to another

Interior Architecture Nonresidential interior design that includes remodeling and working with building systems

Interior Elevation A straight-on view of the surface of an interior wall or walls of a building

Interior Trim Construction term used to denote all interior moldings and baseboards

Ionic Column Classical Greek architectural style column with a scroll-shaped capital

Isometric Drawing A drawing drafted at a 30-degree angle from the horizontal plane and giving equal emphasis to all visible surfaces; all vertical lines remain vertical and all parallel lines parallel

J

Jalousie Window A window made of long, narrow, horizontal panes of hinged glass

Jamb The side and top lining of a doorway, window, or other structural element

Joist A horizontal structural component supporting either the floor or ceiling construction

Junction Box Container for electrical junctions, usually intended to conceal them from sight

L

Landing A flat area either at the end of stairs or between flights of stairs

Lath Thin strip of wood laid parallel and nailed into the studs of a building; walls are plastered over the lath

Lathwork Panels or grids constructed with narrow bands of lath; they often are used as screens or decorative elements

Lattice A panel made of metal or wood bands interlaced to form a grid with even spacing

Layout Defining spaces for specific purposes

Lead-Holder A device that holds different leads for drawing; also known as a mechanical pencil

Legend Box The area containing symbols used in a drawing along with their definitions

Line Weight The lightness or darkness of a line drawn in drafting technique

Lintel The horizontal member above a door or window or between columns

Louvered door Door made up of louvered panels

Louvers Horizontal slats used in a shutter, screen, or window, sloped to control the movement of light and air

Luminaire A lighting unit consisting of one or more electric lamps with all of the necessary parts and wiring

M

Mantel The ledge above and trim around the opening of a fireplace

Masonry Any building material that is bonded together to form a construction element, such as stone, concrete, etc.

Materials and Finishes Board Board used to illustrate the materials and finishes selected for a particular design

Mechanical Pencil A mechanical device shaped like a pencil that holds lead for drawing

Medium Line Weight Line of secondary significance drawn in a medium weight to designate elements in a drawing

Millwork Finish woodwork or carpentry done off site in a mill and delivered to the construction site

Molding A trim or finishing piece to cover joists or edges; moldings can be plain or ornate

Mullion A vertical piece in an opening dividing the space, used in windows to form divisions

Muntin The small bar separating glass panes in a window sash

Mylar A transparent film (paper) used in drafting to show layers or different colors possible to use in any given situation

N **Newel Post** The post at the end of a stair railing or balustrade

Niche A recess in a wall often used to display art

Nosing The rounded edge of a tread. See also Bullnose.

O **Open Floor Plan** The concept in interior design and architectural planning that leaves the spaces open without using walls to delineate them, allowing spaces to be more flexible

Orthographic Drawings See Plan Drawing, Section, and Elevation

Overlay Drafting Drafting technique that involves placing several layers of tracing paper one on top of the other to develop a drawing concept

P **Palladian Window** An arched window with windows on either side

Paneled Door A door formed with rails, stiles, and panels for architectural detailing

Parallel Rule A straight-edged rule attached to a drafting table or to a board by wires, used to draw horizontal lines; a parallel rule also is used in conjunction with triangles to draw vertical lines

Parquet Floor Hardwood floor laid in small rectangular or square patterns instead of long strips

Partition Wall Non-load-bearing interior wall used to divide space

Pendants Type of lighting hung from the ceiling, smaller than a chandelier

Permit Document issued by local, county, state, or federal government to authorize specific work on a building

Perspective Sketch A 3-D sketch or rendering of an interior or exterior space drawn to vanishing points in a perspective manner

Pilaster A flat, decorative column that also offers structural support

Plan Drawing A flat 2-D scaled drawing of a space looking down directly from above

Plasterboard Sheetrock or gypsum board made of pulverized gypsum rock and used to finished the interior walls of a structure; also known as drywall

Plate Rail A shelf used to display plates or small collectibles, usually placed above wainscoting

Plywood Wood product made of thin sheets of wood glued together in layers

Poché Practice of darkening areas on a drawing to aid in the readability of the drawing; the filled or hatched portion of an architectural drawing used to show solid walls

Pocket Door A door that slides into a compartment recessed into a wall and is thereby hidden from view

Post Wood placed vertically as a structural column

Profiling Darkening the outline of part of a floor plan to emphasize the shape

R **Reflected Ceiling Plan** Drawing drafted to indicate the placement of ceiling fixtures, beams, tiles, and electrical outlets

Rendering A term used to denote an elaborate finished drawing used in presentation drafting, an artist's concept, or a perspective drawing

Reproduction Drafting Any form of reproduction to aid in the drafting process

Reprographics Includes all techniques used for reproducing 2-D original drawings

Riser The vertical component of a stair between two treads

S **Scale** The reduced measurement representing a larger measurement, e.g., 1/4" = 1'-0"

Schedule The key or chart that indicates the finish material used on walls, floors, and ceiling and/or lists doors and windows and/or lighting and electrical

Schematic Drawings Beginning or initial drawings or sketches drawn freehand to show relationship of areas

Sconce A wall-mounted lighting fixture

Section A drawing depicting a structure as if it had been sliced through, showing the internal elements of the structure

Shake Shingles Roof shingles made of wood, slightly irregular in width, that generally weather to a gray tone in time

Shed Ceiling A ceiling that slopes in only one direction

Shingles Wood, tile, or asbestos components used as a finish material on angled roofs

Shop Drawings Drawings prepared by the contractor, subcontractor, or manufacturer showing detailed sections of the work to be fabricated and installed

Sill The lower structure of an opening, across the bottom, e.g., a door or window sill

Site Plan A drawing that shows where a building is situated on the land or lot, including the legal boundaries and hookups

Sketch A quick and sometimes rough drawing or illustration of a proposed space or detail of a given space

Soffit The underside of a roof overhang or of another building component, such as an arch, stairway, or cornice, often used as a location for mounting lighting fixtures

Space Planning The process of organizing spaces to meet certain needs, properly allocating spaces to create workable floor plans

Spiral Staircase Staircase working similar to a corkscrew

Stair Tread The horizontal surface of a stair run

Stairway One or more flights of stairs with landings

Stipple The technique of drawing dots in order to define an area in a drawing, e.g., to indicate carpet

Stool The horizontal interior trim component of the casing below a window

Studs (or Stud Wall) The vertical constituent making up the main framework of a wall

Surround The noncombustible material separating the opening of the fireplace from the wall and/or mantel

T **Technical Drawings** Floor plans, elevations, and detailed drawings showing architectural detail

Title Block The part of a drawing that lists the general information about the project—client name, project name, date, scale, type of drawing

Toe Space (or Toe Kick) Recess at the base of cabinetry

Tread The horizontal section of the stair one steps on

T-Square Drafting implement in the shape of a T, used to draft horizontal lines or used as a base to use triangles and other lines

U **Universal Design** Approach to design creating spaces that can be accessed and utilized by all individuals, regardless of age, size, abilities, or disabilities

V **Vellum** The grade of drafting paper, thicker than tracing paper, often used for presentation drawings

Vertical lines Up-and-down lines that raise the eye and bring decorum and formality into interiors

W **Wainscot** Wooden wall paneling on the lower portion of an interior wall, the finish of which generally is different from the portion directly above, e.g., wood versus plaster

Water Closet A room containing a toilet; a bathroom; a toilet

Windowsill The horizontal ridge or shelf beneath the glass, usually part of the window frame

Working Drawings The final drawings used to obtain bids and create a contract

Z **Zero Clearance Fireplace** A fireplace unit that can be placed into combustible walls allowing no clearance